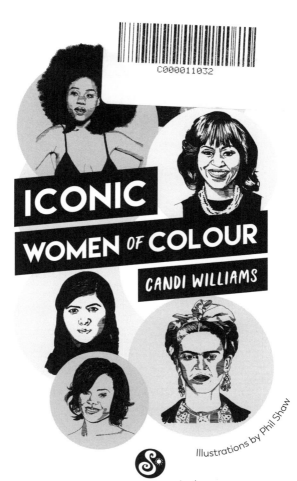

ICONIC

WOMEN OF COLOUR

CANDI WILLIAMS

Illustrations by Phil Shaw

summersdale

ICONIC WOMEN OF COLOUR

An Hachette UK Company
www.hachette.co.uk

Summersdale Publishers Ltd
Part of Octopus Publishing Group Limited
Carmelite House
50 Victoria Embankment
LONDON
EC4Y 0DZ
UK

www.summersdale.com

Printed and bound in Malta

ISBN: 978-1-78685-778-1

This little book is dedicated to anyone who's ever been told they're too much of something – "too fat", "too flat", "too dark", "too loud" – or made to feel "not good enough".

Also, to my beautiful little sisters and princesses: Angelic Afiya, Powerful Parice, Radiant Rubey and Kick-ass Koko.

And last, but never least, my mum – an extraordinary wonder woman who made the world a better place just by being in it. Rest in peace angel; you are forever my number one inspiration.

CONTENTS

INTRODUCTION

Being a woman isn't easy. Throughout history, we've had a patriarchal ceiling imposed upon us, yet century by century we've continued to kick ass, break down boundaries and shun suppressive stereotypes.

In this book you'll find the stories of 38 wonderful women of colour. Women who have had to fight to be heard. To vote. To work. To learn. To love. To be independent. To have the power to say "no". To change perceptions. To pave the way for future generations.

None of these amazing women look the same and they all have their own unique stories. But every one is beautiful, brave and brilliant. Just like you.

So, next time the world tries to put you down, let these stories be a reminder that you are strong, you are powerful, you are worthy. And you got this.

Let's keep changing the world and making history, together.

ALICE WALKER

1944–PRESENT

HER SUPERPOWERS:

Writer and womanist, award winner and activist, it's the amazing Alice Walker.

HER INCREDIBLE STORY

Her book *The Color Purple* has been described as one of the best-loved novels of all time. But what's the story behind the author?

Alice Walker grew up in Georgia. She was blinded in one eye at a young age by a BB gun, but this didn't stop her love of reading and writing. She secured a place at the only high school open to black people in her area and graduated with the highest ranking in her class. Her academic excellence landed her a scholarship to study at a nearby college.

She continued to excel academically but the college years weren't perfect for Alice. She fell pregnant in her senior year and felt lost, confused and suicidal. As such, she decided to have an abortion – something that left her suffering from ongoing anxiety and depression.

In 1965, Alice graduated from college and also met her first husband, Melvyn Rosenman Leventhal, a Jewish civil rights lawyer. They relocated to Jackson and became the first interracial couple to be legally married in Mississippi, where they had a daughter named Rachel. Married life wasn't all butterflies and bliss though – the couple were continually threatened and harassed by small-minded folk, including the Ku Klux Klan.

After graduating, Walker went on to work for the NAACP (National Association for the Advancement of Colored People) and teach a Black Women's

Writers course. She wrote the bestselling novel *The Color Purple* in a year, living in a rented house with just "one big room and a mattress on the floor". It was published in 1982 and won a Pulitzer Prize the next year, making Alice Walker the first black woman to win this award. Hoorah! For anyone who hasn't read it, it's a complete classic. The beautifully written story focuses on strong female characters dealing with the daily struggles and oppression of 1930s southern America. As well as race, it openly explores sexuality; two of the main female characters fall deeply in love. Alice Walker herself identifies as bisexual and had a relationship with Tracy Chapman in 1990, which she describes as "delicious, lovely and wonderful". The novel was made into both a musical and award-winning film, produced by Steven Spielberg and starring Oprah Winfrey and Whoopi Goldberg.

Nowadays, this queen continues to be a devout activist (and kick-ass writer). She's campaigned for women's rights and against female genital mutilation and the blockade of Gaza. What a woman.

HER AWESOME ACHIEVEMENTS

➔ First black woman to receive a Pulitzer Prize for Fiction in 1983.

➔ Coined the word "womanist" meaning "a black feminist or feminist of colour" in 1983.

➔ Awarded the LennonOno Grant for Peace in 2010.

➔ Inducted into the California Hall of Fame in 2003.

"I WAS ORDERED IMMEDIATELY TO THE BACK OF THE BUS BECAUSE A WHITE WOMAN COMPLAINED TO THE WHITE BUS DRIVER... I HAD BEEN WRITING POETRY SINCE I WAS NINE, BUT I REALIZED THEN I WOULD NEVER HAVE THE LUXURY OF ONLY WRITING POETRY; THAT I WOULD HAVE TO BE POLITICALLY ACTIVE TO ACHIEVE ENOUGH FREEDOM TO WRITE AT ALL."

ARETHA FRANKLIN

1942–2018

HER SUPERPOWERS:

Described by Bill Clinton as "bringing sunshine to a rainy day and tenderness to a hardened heart", Aretha Franklin was a soul superstar, a feminist icon who left a powerful legacy.

HER INCREDIBLE STORY

Aretha Franklin sang from the heart into the hearts of others. Her hits earned her the title of the Queen of Soul and, beyond the bouffant and uplifting dance moves, were filled with strong and empowering messages. "Think", "Sisters are Doing it for Themselves" and "Respect" are all calls to ladies to come together, realize their worth and demand respect.

Aretha was born in Memphis, Tennessee in 1942 to a Baptist minister father and piano-playing vocalist mother. At just 14, she recorded her first gospel collection in her father's church.

Fame came quickly and five years later, Aretha signed to Columbia Records. She had a number of minor hits with the label and married her manager that same year. It wasn't until Aretha joined Atlantic Records in 1967, however, that her success exploded. She was invited to the reputable FAME Studios to record but the experience didn't go as smoothly as her beautiful voice. Her husband (and manager), Ted White, didn't see eye to eye with the owner of the studios, Rick Hall, and Aretha found herself caught in the middle of a heated argument while trying to record her first album. She didn't let it stop her. In that session, she recorded one of the biggest hits of her career, "I Never Loved a Man the Way I Love You". She was honoured with a day named after her by long-standing friend, Martin Luther King, that same year.

It wasn't long before Aretha's soulful music started a movement. Her cover of Otis Redding's "Respect" fast became an anthem for civil rights and feminism in the late 1960s. Women who'd felt oppressed and stereotyped for years were suddenly standing up together against huge issues like domestic abuse, fair pay and abortion rights. They were, indeed, demanding some well-deserved R.E.S.P.E.C.T.

She separated from Ted White in 1969 and stepped up her civil rights activism. Aretha funded numerous protests and rallies and used her lyrics to tell a story of oppression and hope. In 1972, she released two powerful albums, *Young and Gifted and Black* and the double-platinum *Amazing Grace*, which became the biggest selling album of her career.

From gospel to soul, Aretha's vocal performances continued to wow audiences until the day she died. And when she passed away from cancer in the summer of 2018, people across the world – from Barack Obama to Stevie Wonder – shared amazing stories of admiration and tribute. Barbra Streisand said, "It's difficult to conceive of a world without her. Not only was she a uniquely brilliant singer, but her commitment to civil rights made an indelible impact on the world."

The one and only Queen of Soul will be sorely missed but never forgotten in our hearts and playlists.

HER AWESOME ACHIEVEMENTS

➔ Achieved 17 Top Ten US Chart Hits.

➔ Won 18 Grammy Awards.

➔ Sang at Barack Obama's inauguration.

➔ Given an award by Martin Luther King.

➔ Youngest person ever to receive the Kennedy Center Honors.

"DON'T SAY ARETHA IS MAKING A COMEBACK, BECAUSE I'VE NEVER BEEN AWAY!"

"NEVER ANSWER TO A HAND CLAP, A WHISTLE OR SOMEONE SNAPPING THEIR FINGERS AT YOU. YOU ARE NOT A DOG."

BESSIE COLEMAN

1892–1926

HER SUPERPOWERS:

The sky most certainly wasn't the limit for Bessie Coleman, the first African-American female pilot.

HER INCREDIBLE STORY

Becoming a pilot is no mean feat. It takes years of training, learning and proving yourself. So you can imagine how challenging it must have been for a young black woman back in the early 1900s.

These odds didn't stop young Bessie Coleman from following her dream. She grew up in a segregated small town in Texas where most of her home life was spent handwashing clothes, fetching clean water or walking 6.5 km (4 miles) back and forth to school every day. At 12 years old, Bessie received a scholarship to study at the Missionary Baptist School. This gave her a taste for education and, at 18, she took all the money she'd saved up from cotton work and went off to university. She was there a term before her money ran out and she had to return home. But Bessie knew it wouldn't be this way forever.

Bored of living in a small town, Bessie decided to move to Chicago, where her brothers lived. They had just returned from the First World War and were full of stories of France and how women could fly there. Working as a manicurist in a barber's shop at the time, Bessie's mind was opened – she found herself dreaming of being able to fly planes and add some adventure to her life. So she applied to every flying school she could find. They all rejected her, as American flight schools didn't allow women – or black people – in at the time. Never one to give up,

Bessie signed up for French lessons and then moved to Paris just months later.

She enrolled in a French flying school and completed the ten-month pilot's course in just seven months. And in 1921, Bessie became the first African-American woman to receive a pilot's licence. She specialized in stunt flying and her air shows drew crowds far and wide. She soon became an international celebrity.

Bessie used her platform to stand up against discrimination. She had big dreams to open her own flying school for other women of colour. But when rehearsing for an air show in 1926, she was thrown tragically from her plane due to a mechanical fault and died instantly – at just 34 years old.

Gone but far, far from forgotten, Bessie's legacy lives on. Today, scholarships are given out in her honour and flying clubs founded in her name to promote diversity in aviation. Her tenacity and refusal to give up has flown the flag for many other women of colour to reach for their dreams. Thank you, Queen Bess.

HER AWESOME ACHIEVEMENTS

→ First African-American woman to receive an international pilot's licence.

→ Several Bessie Coleman Scholarship Awards have been given out in her memory.

→ Inducted into the National Aviation Hall of Fame in 2006.

→ In 2015, Orlando (where Bessie died) renamed West Washington Street "Bessie Coleman Street" to honour her.

"THE AIR IS THE ONLY PLACE FREE FROM PREJUDICES."

"I KNEW WE HAD NO AVIATORS... AND I KNEW THAT RACE NEEDED TO BE REPRESENTED... SO I THOUGHT IT MY DUTY TO RISK MY LIFE TO LEARN AVIATION."

BEYONCÉ

1981–PRESENT

HER SUPERPOWERS:

The world's seen her grow – and glow – from Destiny's Child to Dream Girl to wife, mother and political activist. And there are oh-so-many beautiful reasons to adore Beyoncé.

HER INCREDIBLE STORY

Queen Bey. She's known for her fierce outfits, killer choreography and selling out stadiums worldwide. But there's a lot more to this mega-babe than her killer moves.

Beyoncé Giselle Knowles was at a dance class when her singing talent was first discovered. Her instructor started humming a song and she finished it off, high notes and all. Shortly after, she met Kelly Rowland, LeToya Luckett and LaTavia Roberson and started the group Girl's Tyme. They competed in *Star Search* (an old *X Factor*-like show). Although they didn't win, it boosted their profile and Beyoncé's father, Mathew Knowles, gave up his job to manage the group.

By 1999, they'd changed their name to Destiny's Child, signed a record deal, sold over eight million album copies and won two Grammys. But Bey grew depressed. The band dynamics hit tough times and LeToya and LaTavia were replaced by Michelle Williams and Farrah Franklin. Bey's mother, Tina, helped her overcome depression and Destiny's Child went on to be one of the best-selling groups of all time.

In 2003, Queen Bey started her solo career. Now – seven albums, three beautiful children and 490 international tour dates later – she's the highest paid black musical artist in history. She's sold over 100 million records worldwide and is MTV Video Music

Awards' most awarded artist in history. In 2016, she changed the game with her unforgettable visual album, *Lemonade*. It's over an hour of strikingly honest vocals, thought-provoking videography and hard-hitting nods to Malcolm X, Trayvon Martin, Blue Ivy and, of course, "Becky with the good hair".

Her fearless risk-taking and fierce strength are a constant reminder that women can do whatever they put their minds to. From break-ups to breakdowns, her songs have an unrivalled ability to help you find strength and feel like a queen again.

She came under media scrutiny for using the term "feminist" in one of her tours, because of her marriage and sex symbol status. But who said you can't be married, glamorous *and* a feminist? You can and Bey is.

She's raising three young feminists of her own too. After suffering a miscarriage, which she describes as "the saddest thing" she's ever gone through, Bey gave birth to Blue Ivy in 2012 and twins Rumi and Sir in 2017. Of all her accomplishments, it was her "proudest moment" to date. She survived postnatal depression with Blue and harrowing health complications with the twins and is now just embracing her "mommy pouch" and "FUPA" – fat upper pubic area (her words, not ours).

Post-birth or post-gig, natural or glam, this queen radiates beauty – inside and out – while reminding us all who runs the world. You glow, Bey.

HER AWESOME ACHIEVEMENTS

→ Her self-titled album, *Beyoncé*, became the fastest-selling album in iTunes history.

→ She was the first female solo artist to headline Glastonbury in over 20 years (in 2011).

→ Her #BEYGOOD initiative and charitable work has raised millions of dollars to help young girls facing death because they want to learn, and stop women dying during childbirth because of poor healthcare conditions.

→ She performed at both of Barack Obama's inaugurations. Michelle and Barack were also spotted dancing away at her OTRII tour.

→ She was ranked twice by Forbes as "the most powerful female in entertainment".

"ANY OTHER WOMAN WHO HAS TO GO TO WORK AND PICK UP THE KIDS AND MAKE DINNER... THAT'S WAY HARDER THAN WHAT I HAVE TO DO."

CARMEN PEREZ

1977–PRESENT

HER SUPERPOWERS:

The Women's March co-founder who's been marching America towards social justice and violence prevention for 20 years. She's all kinds of awesome.

HER INCREDIBLE STORY

Carmen Perez has been fighting for social justice for 20 years – and she doesn't look a day over 30.

Born in 1977, Carmen was the youngest of five siblings living in a Latino home. The small Californian town they lived in was rife with violence, gangs and police brutality, so Carmen focused on basketball in her early years "as a positive alternative". At 16, her world changed forever when her sister, Patricia, was killed in a car crash. They'd been raised like twins and shared a room their whole lives. Carmen buried Patricia on her 17th birthday. It was a life-changing moment. Later, when the police asked their father if he wanted to press charges, he replied "I will never take another mother's child away". From that day, Carmen dedicated her life to social justice, community activism and making a difference.

Knowing that she wanted to help people, Carmen went to study Psychology at University of California Santa Cruz. It was there that she realized what was going on back home – the excessive police brutality and violence – wasn't normal. It was an example of racial profiling and a symptom of an "inherently racist (in)justice system". Keen to change this, she started working with young juvenile offenders and set up a young people's mentoring programme. In 2003, she was elected as Chair of the Latino Affairs Commission of Santa Cruz.

Her work over the years has, quite literally, changed people's lives. Carmen has spent time in prisons across the globe, understanding the "why" behind people's crimes to inform prevention techniques. In 2010, she became Executive Director for The Gathering for Justice – an organization that works to stop police brutality and child incarceration. This led to her co-founding the Justice League, an organization that brings criminal justice experts, ex-prisoners and policymakers together around the table to help reform the criminal and social justice system.

Most recently, in 2017, this wonder woman co-chaired the Women's March – hosted the day after Trump was inaugurated. She wanted to show him that women were "working in unity" – and it worked: 470,000 attended the march (compared to 160,000 at Trump's inauguration).

So, what next for Perez the game-changer? Lots. Carmen's keen to get more Latino people involved in social action. She also wants to strengthen relationships with the trans community and make sure all marches are super accessible to attend. And her five-year plan? To "have a woman candidate in the White House who represents our issues".

We think we might just know the perfect person for the job...

HER AWESOME ACHIEVEMENTS

→ Co-founder of the Women's March, attended by 470,000 people in 2017.

→ Executive Director of The Gathering for Justice, promoting peace and justice across the globe.

→ Named one of *Fortune*'s Top 50 World Leaders.

→ Won a Gutsy Award from the National Juvenile Justice Network.

→ Led March2Justice, a 400 km (250 mile) march through five states to draw Congressional attention to legislation reforms that confront police violence.

"MY CAREER AND PATH CHOSE ME AT A VERY YOUNG AGE AFTER THE SUDDEN DEATH OF MY SISTER, WHICH ACTIVATED MY LIFE'S PURPOSE TO CHANGE THE WORLD... STARTING IN MY OWN COMMUNITY."

MOKGADI CASTER SEMENYA

1991–PRESENT

HER SUPERPOWERS:

The record-breaking, boundary-defying, Olympic-winning runner who's had her gender publicly questioned for years – simply for being a super-fast runner. Caster Semenya is amazing (exactly as she is).

HER INCREDIBLE STORY

Winning a gold medal at a world-renowned sporting event is an incredible achievement. Beating your personal best is even greater cause for congratulation. Or, at least it should have been for Caster Semenya.

But the events following Semenya's win at the 2009 African Junior Championships were far from the celebrations you might expect for a runner who had just broken a world record for the 800 m race.

Instead of being hailed a hero, Semenya was accused of being a fraud. The International Association of Athletics Federation (IAAF) questioned if she was really a female because of her super-speedy performance. While it might sound shocking, it was taken seriously and they made Semenya take a sex verification test. The results were never published but in November 2009, the IAAF officially announced that Semenya could keep her medal and award. Shortly after, she was cleared to compete again.

This was a huge ordeal for the just 18-year-old to go through. Imagine being forced to justify your gender and having your name dragged through the headlines simply for being brilliant at your sport. Thankfully, Semenya received overwhelming support across the globe. From South Africa's Minister of Sports and Recreation, Makhenkesi Stofile, to basketballer Michael Jordan, people spoke out in her favour and threw shade at the IAAF's handling of the situation. This spurred her on to take legal action and she appointed a law firm to protect her human and civil rights.

Refusing to let the negativity get in the way of what she loves most, Semenya has sprinted from success to success since 2009. In 2016, she became the first person to win the 400 m, 800 m and 1500 m titles in the South African Championships and won gold in the 800 m at the Rio Olympics the same year. Caster Semenya is nothing short of remarkable, but with every victory has come more scrutiny.

In 2018, the IAAF announced a change in rules that meant women with particularly high levels of testosterone would be forced to take medication to lower their levels – or race against men – to compete in the 400 m, 800 m or 1500 m races. As these are Semenya's famous races, many thought this was directly aimed at her. How did she take the news? With strength and dignity, as ever. Instead of feeling deflated, Semenya is taking legal action against the IAAF to protect the rights of other women. She's also shared her story through a Nike ad, where she boldly and beautifully lets the world know that she was "born to do this".

Thank goodness she was, because the sporting world is a richer, more wonderful place with this legendary lady in it. Go, Semenya – and shame on the shamers.

HER AWESOME ACHIEVEMENTS

→ Fourth fastest female 800 m runner of all time, with a personal best time of 1:54.25.

→ Won gold for women's 800 m at 2016 Olympics in Rio.

→ Awarded South African Sportswoman of the Year at SA Sports Awards, 2012.

→ A spotlight feature in Nike's 30th "Just Do It" anniversary campaign in 2018.

→ Personal best for the 400 m of 49.62 seconds.

"WOULD IT BE EASIER FOR YOU IF I WASN'T SO FAST? WOULD IT BE SIMPLER IF I STOPPED WINNING? WOULD YOU BE MORE COMFORTABLE IF I WAS LESS PROUD? WOULD YOU PREFER IF I HADN'T WORKED SO HARD, OR JUST DIDN'T RUN? OR CHOSE A DIFFERENT SPORT? OR STOPPED AT MY FIRST STEP? THAT'S TOO BAD BECAUSE I WAS BORN TO DO THIS."

CHIDERA "THE SLUMFLOWER" EGGERUE

1994-PRESENT

HER SUPERPOWERS:

Some say she's "categorically one of the coolest people in Britain". Others call her "this generation's agony aunt". Her name? Chidera. Her superpowers? Inspiring a generation.

HER INCREDIBLE STORY

Saggy boobs matter – it's a hashtag you might have seen shimmying its way around Instagram. And it's all thanks to the game-changing Miss Eggerue.

Her fabulous social media feed is full of amazing adventures, epic outfits and vibrant videos. But what stands out most about Chidera is her honesty. Unlike many insta-famous faces, there's no air of unattainable perfection or filtered fakery. She shares the good days and the bad, and balances blue weaves and bright eyeshadow with make-up-free looks and self-love pep talks.

Far from just a social media superstar, Chidera Eggerue is an author of two books, a radio show host, an award-winning blogger and a "millennial mastermind" (*Vogue*). That's no mean feat of achievements for less than a quarter of a decade on this Earth. But it hasn't always been body love and social stuff. Chidera grew up in Peckham pre-gentrification. Her pseudonym, "The Slumflower", describes her blossoming in an area that isn't always associated with thriving. Growing up, she was far from confident. Many of her teen years were spent picking holes in her appearance and dreaming of a boob job, as her cleavage didn't fit the perfectly pert images from the glossy magazines. Eventually, she decided to make a stand.

The day Chidera decided to embrace her natural boobs was a turning point in more than just her own life. She'd been flicking through photos from a night out and found a "happy" one she wanted to post, but felt concerned about people thinking her boobs looked saggy. Thankfully, she did it anyway accompanied by the hashtag #saggyboobsmatter. At the time, she had no idea it'd be the start of a huge movement, but today, the hashtag has over 10,000 Instagram posts from fans around the world. It's inspired women everywhere to feel comfortable in their skin and reassured them that there's no one-size-fits-all rule when it comes to being beautiful.

"We do not exist for the consumption of men", Chidera reminds us. "If I had seen women with saggy boobs being glorified for their beauty, I wouldn't have developed a complex as a very young teen. This is exactly why this representation is important."

Her debut book, *What a Time to Be Alone,* is filled with mindset-changing inspiration to help women understand their worth, stop comparing themselves to others and realize that their true beauty isn't defined by filters and likes. And amid writing best-selling books and blogs, and inspiring a generation, she still makes time for a cheeky Nando's.

Queen Chidera, take a bow (and let those boobs jiggle free).

HER AWESOME ACHIEVEMENTS

→ Her book became a *Sunday Times* bestseller within just a week of being released.

→ Named one of *Vogue*'s Six Women to Read in 2018.

→ One of the faces of Adidas's 2018 campaign, baring her natural beauty on billboards all over the UK and beyond.

→ Presented a TEDx talk on body positivity and female empowerment.

→ Met and spent time with Oprah – a total highlight for her!

"SADLY, NO AMOUNT OF 'PERFECTION' CAN MAKE YOU COMPLETELY HAPPY WITH YOURSELF. INSTEAD OF CHASING EMPTY IDEALS, WHY NOT FOCUS ON BUILDING A RELATIONSHIP WITH THE PARTS OF YOURSELF THAT YOU'VE BEEN TAUGHT TO HATE?"

CHIMAMANDA NGOZI ADICHIE

1977–PRESENT

HER SUPERPOWERS:

Writer Ngozi Adichie doesn't mince her words; she strings them together in a beautiful way that moves hearts and minds.

HER INCREDIBLE STORY

We teach girls to shrink themselves, to make themselves smaller.

We say to girls: you can have ambition, but not too much.

Her words have echoed stages around the world. They've emblazoned sweaters, tees and babygros and filled best-selling books. Chimamanda Ngozi Adichie is a writer, storyteller, teacher, feminist, modern-day activist and so much more.

She's a proud Nigerian, who "didn't think of herself as black" until she moved to America to study at 19. It was the first time she felt that she had to fit a tick box – literally. A penny-drop moment was when a college professor asked who'd written an essay, as it was the best in the class. When Chimamanda raised her hand, he looked surprised. It was surprising for her too. Coming from a country where being black *and* academically superior was commonplace, this experience was an eye-opener. She started to think deeply and differently about identity – a topic that's inspired much of her written work.

Today, Chimamanda's experience is that many people find conversations about gender and sexism more "uncomfortable" than those about racism. Her book *We Should All Be Feminists* has played a pivotal role towards inspiring a nation on what feminism really is: believing in the social, political and economic equality of the sexes. That doesn't mean hating men or being "bitter". It means "a fairer world of happier men and happier women". A world where "men don't feel their self-worth is diminished if they're not in power" and where gender issues can be discussed rather than swept under the carpet. Chimamanda manages to sum it up in a way that everyone can understand. And, written by a mum raising a young daughter, her book *Dear Ijeawele: A Feminist Manifesto in Fifteen Suggestions* offers parents with a witty and insightful manifesto for raising a baby girl as a feminist.

What would she be up to if not speaking out about the world's big issues? What she does best: storytelling. Stories have always been Chimamanda's passion. In 2001, she received a degree "with the highest honour" in Communications and Political Sciences, before going on to do a Masters in Creative Writing and another in African Studies at Yale. And, on top of writing bestselling books such as *Americanah*, she's taught creative writing across the world and spoken out about cultural underrepresentation in books.

Whether it's conjuring up beautiful works of fiction or sharing feminism in simple terms, Chimamanda is a literary hero as well as one of the greatest womanists of our time. And she doesn't plan on stopping anytime soon (thank goodness for that).

HER AWESOME ACHIEVEMENTS

→ One of *Foreign Policy Magazine's* Top Global Thinkers of 2013.

→ Her talk *The Danger of a Single Story* is one of the top 10 most viewed TED talks of all time, with over 15 million views.

→ Her book *Americanah* was picked as the winning novel for the "One Book, One New York" community reading initiative that encourages all city residents to read the same book.

→ She was elected to the American Academy of Arts and Sciences in 2017, one of the highest honours for intellectuals in the US.

→ She also received the MacArthur Fellowship – known as the "Genius Grant" – for individuals who show "extraordinary originality and dedication in their creative pursuits".

"CULTURE DOES NOT MAKE PEOPLE. PEOPLE MAKE CULTURE."

CORAZON AQUINO

1933–2009

HER SUPERPOWERS:

From proud homemaker and mum to President of the Philippines, kamusta (hello) Corazon Aquino.

HER INCREDIBLE STORY

The Philippines is known for its tantalizing tropics and breathtaking beaches. In 1986, Corazon Aquino put it on the map for game-changing politics when she became the country's first female president.

In the 1960s and 1970s, Corazon (fondly known as Cory) was a proud homemaker, mum and wife. She enjoyed raising her five children, cooking tasty fare and caring for her bonsai trees. Her husband Benigno's career had gone from strength to strength over the years – progressing from budding journalist to the nation's youngest senator. Cory had supported him at every step of the way.

Things took a turn in 1972 when President Marcos, Benigno's rival, declared martial law in the country. He immediately called for Senator Benigno's arrest and, much to Cory's heartbreak, her husband was imprisoned and sentenced to death by firing squad.

Suddenly, Corazon – a lady who rarely left the house – found herself campaigning for her husband's right to live and giving political speeches. When Benigno suffered a heart attack in prison, he refused to be treated by Filipino doctors (in case of foul play) and was granted treatment in America. Corazon and the family moved with him, but, in 1983, he returned to the Philippines alone and was tragically assassinated at Manila airport.

Benigno's assassination caused uproar worldwide. Corazon became more politically active and championed the People Power Revolution, calling for peace in the Philippines. When Marcos called an election in 1985, there was one name on everyone's lips: Corazon. The country gathered over a million signatures endorsing her to run for president and she reluctantly agreed. That day, she changed the game; a kind-hearted, strong woman in a political climate of greed, violence and coercion.

Corazon was sworn in shortly after and became the Philippines' first female president. The first thing she did? Set up a taskforce with the main aim of investigating and recovering ill-gotten wealth from the previous presidential regime. She called it the Presidential Commission on Good Government. Corazon also abolished the violent martial law constitution in favour of a new Freedom Constitution. She also promoted new policies such as "The Family Code 1987", which brought about fairer, more equal rights in marriage and divorce.

As well as dealing with billions of dollars of debt racked up by the previous regime, she worked hard to tackle mass poverty – facing attacks and sabotages from Marcos's government friends throughout.

Her time in office was known as "the peaceful revolutionary". But Corazon famously underplayed the incredible work she did. For her, it was about peace and honesty not greed and wealth. And when her term came to an end, she graciously handed over to the new president and drove off in her humble Toyota. She continued to live her values through retirement, running anti-violence think tanks and supporting peaceful protests, before passing away from bowel cancer in 2009.

Rest peacefully, you magnificent boss lady.

HER AWESOME ACHIEVEMENTS

➔ Became the Philippines' first female president in 1986.

➔ Founded and chaired the Benigno S. Aquino, Jr. Foundation, set up in her husband's honour.

➔ Named one of the 20 Most Influential Asians of the twentieth century by *Time* magazine.

➔ Received J. William Fulbright award for International Understanding in 1996.

➔ Lifelong member of the Council for Woman World Leaders.

"POLITICS MUST NOT REMAIN A BASTION OF MALE DOMINANCE, FOR THERE IS MUCH THAT WOMEN CAN BRING INTO POLITICS THAT WOULD MAKE OUR WORLD A KINDER, GENTLER PLACE FOR HUMANITY TO THRIVE IN."

DIANE ABBOTT

1953–PRESENT

HER SUPERPOWERS:

*She's been championing policies that put people –
not politics – first for over 30 years, shaping a legacy
that goes far beyond statistics and soundbites.*

HER INCREDIBLE STORY

It's a name you might well have seen on TV or heard on the radio over recent years. But Diane Abbott is so much more than a face on our post-Brexit vote screens or a media-splashed headline.

She's a change-maker. A groundbreaker. A tireless fighter for human rights. And a black woman who has defied all odds to achieve amazing things and help the people and communities around her.

The Brexit broadcasts weren't the first time Diane has faced criticism or doubters. As a child, she was the only black student in her grammar school and distinctly remembers her teacher handing back marked essays in her favourite English class. Having worked super hard, Diane had her hopes pinned on an A. So, when the teacher dished out the A+s, As, Bs and even Cs with nothing for Diane, she became disheartened. After class, her teacher picked up Diane's A-grade essay and sternly asked: "Where did you copy this from?" Diane was heartbroken and for the rest of the year, she wrote with slightly less brilliance so she would not to be embarrassed again.

Thankfully, for Hackney and for the Home Office, Diane didn't let this dampen her dreams. Even when a sixth form teacher tried to crush her ambitions of Oxford or Cambridge by saying "I don't think you're up to it", Diane replied: "But I do, and that's what matters." Months later, she'd passed her entrance exams and become the only black person in the History faculty at Newnham College, Cambridge.

That was a defining moment for Diane. After graduating with a History degree, she worked as a civil servant in the Home Office and served on the National Council for Civil Liberties before becoming the UK's first black female MP in 1987.

Over the last 30 years, Diane has achieved a huge amount – for her community, for London and for people across the UK. As Shadow Minister for Public Health, she continually fought to tackle the government's cuts to children's services, maternity care and much more. She repeatedly stands up for issues that are often swept under the carpet, campaigning against cuts to domestic violence support services and disability and illness benefits. Her work doesn't stop in the UK either. She represents government internationally and has worked closely with other countries to help develop a well-rounded, effective immigration policy.

Throughout everything, MP Diane Abbott hasn't allowed the doubt or negativity of others – from reluctant teachers to racist trolls – to hold her back. She's never given up on her city, her country or her beliefs. So, next time you're feeling like you can't do something, remember Diane's real story, and believe in yourself.

HER AWESOME ACHIEVEMENTS

➜ First black woman elected to Parliament in 1987.

➜ Race Relations Officer at the National Council for Civil Liberties from 1978 to 1980.

➜ Won "Parliamentary Speech of the Year" in the *Spectator* Awards for her speech on civil liberties in the counterterrorism debate in 2008.

➜ Founded the Black Child initiative to raise educational achievements among black kids.

➜ Named "one of Labour's best front bench performers" by *The Telegraph* in 2011.

"THE TRUTH IS: YOU CAN EITHER HAVE AN EFFICIENT, FAIR AND HUMANE IMMIGRATION SYSTEM THAT WORKS FOR US ALL, OR YOU CAN HAVE BASELESS NUMERICAL TARGETS FOR IMMIGRATION AND DEPORTATIONS. YOU CAN'T HAVE BOTH."

BARONESS DOREEN LAWRENCE

1952–PRESENT

HER SUPERPOWERS:

*She's the woman who took on "institutional racism"
in the justice system and won. All hail, Queen Doreen.*

HER INCREDIBLE STORY

Stephen Lawrence. It was the story that shook a nation – and every mother's worst nightmare.

On Thursday, 22 April 1993, 18-year-old Stephen Lawrence was waiting for a bus when he was jumped by a group of men and stabbed to death in a horrific racist attack. The attackers had a history of racist stabbings and dozens of witnesses came forward. But just four months later, all charges were dropped against the suspects.

The lack of justice and police handling of the case was heartbreaking for Stephen's mum, Doreen. Her kind, innocent son had been studying for his A levels with dreams of becoming an architect – dreams stolen from him by dangerous thugs. Doreen and her husband launched a national appeal and set up a fund to pay for further examination of the forensic evidence and interviewing of witnesses. They even visited Nelson Mandela, who offered his full support.

Eventually, Doreen's tireless work started to pay off. The Home Secretary commissioned an inquiry into the police investigation in 1997. The inquiry, conducted by William Macpherson, found "institutional racism" in the police system and blamed "unwitting prejudice, ignorance and racist stereotyping" for the lack of justice in the case. One of Macpherson's recommendations was to abolish the double jeopardy law, which prevented people from being tried again for the same crime once acquitted. This was pivotal, as it would mean the suspects of Stephen's murder could be brought to trial again. The law was finally abolished in 2005.

Thanks to new evidence and Doreen's unwavering determination, she finally got the moment she'd been waiting for. In January 2012, Doreen watched from court as the two thugs that killed her beloved son were sentenced to life in prison. The judge confirmed that the gang attack was committed for "no other reason than racial hatred".

For Doreen, it was a moment of mixed emotions. She was grateful for all the support along the way but also felt that "had the police done their job properly in 1993" she could have spent the time grieving for her son, "not fighting to get his killers to court".

She hasn't stopped fighting against injustice since. Doreen directed Theresa May to commission an investigation into police corruption in 2014 and has sat on numerous panels for the Home Office and Police Service.

She's also raised enough money through the Stephen Lawrence Charitable Trust to give hundreds of young people bursaries to study architecture – just like her son had hoped to. It's safe to say that the British justice system wouldn't be the same today without this lady – a baroness and a mum who never gave up.

Thank you, Doreen. And forever in our hearts, Stephen.

HER AWESOME ACHIEVEMENTS

→ Became Baroness Lawrence of Clarendon, OBE in 2013.

→ Founder and President of the Stephen Lawrence Charitable Trust, which gives bursaries to young people aspiring to be architects.

→ Became Chancellor of De Montfort University in Leicester in 2016.

→ Directed Theresa May to investigate police corruption in 2014 – resulting in a report that highlighted a number of failings.

→ Won a Lifetime Achievement Award at the 14th Pride of Britain Awards in 2012.

"I WOULD LIKE STEPHEN TO BE REMEMBERED AS A YOUNG MAN WHO HAD A FUTURE. HE WAS WELL LOVED AND... DIDN'T DISTINGUISH BETWEEN BLACK OR WHITE. HE SAW PEOPLE AS PEOPLE."

FRIDA KAHLO

1907–1954

HER SUPERPOWERS:

From her appearance to her artwork,
Frida Kahlo is unique. And so is her story.

HER INCREDIBLE STORY

Frida's is a tale of love and pain.

She was born Magdelena Carmen Frida Kahlo y Calderon to photographer parents in La Casa Azul (The Blue House) in Mexico City. At school, she was known for being outspoken, political and rebellious. Her love of painting came about by tragic accident. She was in a bus collision at school when a steel handrail impaled her hip. To ease her boredom as she was bedridden for months, her parents bought her a specially made easel and Frida started painting the subject she knew best – herself.

In 1928, Frida invited fellow artist Diego Rivera to check out her work. He took a shine to more than just her paintings and they married the next year, much to her mother's distaste.

Having moved to America, their love story turned rocky in the 1930s. Frida's ground-breakingly famous portrait *The Two Fridas* shows two versions of Frida sitting next to each other, one holding a small portrait of Diego. There is blood dripping from her veins, demonstrating her pain – which became a regular theme in her art. The portrait also draws upon her identity, with one Frida wearing traditional elaborate European attire of the time and the other in indigenous Mexican clothing.

She became the first twentieth-century Mexican artist to be featured in the Louvre in 1939 when they bought her portrait *The Frame*. Over the next decade, she created some of her most iconic portraits, including *Self-Portrait with Thorn Necklace and Hummingbird*, which highlights her love of animals, and *Self-Portrait with Cropped Hair*, which shows a totally different style for Frida.

It's fair to say that Frida's unique look is as well known as her art. Even if you've never seen one of her portraits, you'll know her face. And can we just take a moment to appreciate those brows?

Illness caught up with Frida in the 1940s. Her spinal problems continued and she grew depressed when her beloved dad died. She channelled the pain into new paintings and spent her last years in America hanging out with Picasso and André Breton before moving back to Mexico to paint and exhibit her work.

She spent many of her final years in hospital – and once famously ordered a four-poster to be craned to a gallery so she could attend her own exhibition.

In June 1954, Frida Kahlo passed away. But her art and style has influenced generations to this day. Madonna has Frida's *My Birth* painting hanging in her home and famously said, "If someone doesn't like this painting, they can't be my friend." From her style to her surrealist paintings, she is one of the greatest icons of all time and it's hard to imagine art history without Ms Kahlo.

HER AWESOME ACHIEVEMENTS

→ Her childhood home, La Casa Azul, was opened to the public in 1958 and is now one of the most popular museums in Mexico City, with around 25,000 monthly visitors.

→ Her hometown also dedicated a park to her, Parque Frida Kahlo, in 1985.

→ Became the first Latin American artist to break the one-million-dollar threshold when *Diego and I* was auctioned at Sotheby's for $1,430,000.

"NOTHING IS WORTH MORE THAN LAUGHTER. IT IS STRENGTH TO LAUGH AND TO ABANDON ONESELF, TO BE LIGHT."

HALLE BERRY

1966–PRESENT

HER SUPERPOWERS:

All hail, Halle Berry: actress, business boss, domestic violence survivor, fitness fanatic.

HER INCREDIBLE STORY

Giving a speech from the Oscars podium must be daunting for anyone. But imagine doing it as the first black woman ever to have picked up the Best Actress Award. Instead of playing it safe with a rehearsed list of professional thank yous, Halle Berry used her record-breaking moment to share an important message. She dedicated the award to the black actresses, present and past, and to "opening doors" for new actresses to achieve what they never thought possible. It was a pivotal moment – especially for someone who had been an unknown actress just ten years before.

Halle was born in Cleveland, Ohio, where she was raised by her mother. Her father left when she was about four but Halle recalls him beating her mother daily, kicking her down the stairs and even hitting her in the head with a wine bottle.

Halle moved to the Big Apple in her early twenties to follow her dream of becoming an actress. It soon became clear that the cash she'd scraped together wasn't going to last in the bright lights of New York City and she found herself sleeping in a homeless shelter for some time. She took it in her stride and "figured it out" by working waitressing jobs until she landed a role on the ABC series *Living Dolls* in 1989.

Things skyrocketed for Halle's acting ambitions in the 1990s and early 2000s when she took on lead roles in hits such as *Boomerang*, *X-Men*, *Swordfish*,

Die Another Day and *Monster's Ball*. She also starred in an ode to one of her idols as Dorothy Dandridge (who was born in the same hospital as Halle), the first black woman to be nominated for the Best Actress Academy Award.

But while things were flourishing professionally, Halle was facing some struggles in her personal life. In 2010, she opened up about the effect her father's domestic abuse had on her boyfriend choices. One ex-boyfriend had hit her so hard it left her 80 per cent deaf in one ear. Ever since, she's worked closely with shelters and charities to support people living through domestic abuse and constantly offered a hearty dose of support and self-belief to women.

In recent years, Halle has taken a breather from the red carpets to focus on herself and her two children. In 2013, her legal action played a key part in legislation being passed in California to stop paparazzi using threatening and aggressive behaviour to secure photos of celebrities' children.

She uses her Instagram as a platform to encourage women to love, protect and value themselves more. And can we just take a minute to appreciate how incredible she looks while doing it all?

HER AWESOME ACHIEVEMENTS

→ First African-American woman to represent the US in the Miss World Competition in 1986.

→ First (and to date only) black woman to receive the Best Actress Award at the Oscars.

→ First celebrity ambassador for the Diabetes Aware campaign.

→ Picked up five awards for her leading actress role in *Monster's Ball* alone.

→ Volunteered at and raised funds for the Jenneuse Center of Domestic Violence Intervention and Protection for over 10 years.

"THERE HAVE BEEN SO MANY PEOPLE WHO HAVE SAID TO ME 'YOU CAN'T DO THAT,' BUT I'VE HAD AN INNATE BELIEF THAT THEY WERE WRONG. BE UNWAVERING AND RELENTLESS IN YOUR APPROACH."

IBTIHAJ MUHAMMAD

1985–PRESENT

HER SUPERPOWERS:

Proud Muslim, game-changing Olympian, fashion business owner – it's the incredible Ibtihaj Muhammad.

HER INCREDIBLE STORY

Olympic fencer Ibtihaj Muhammad is a woman of many firsts. She's the first Muslim American woman to win an Olympic medal, the first US woman to compete in the Olympics wearing a hijab and the first Muslim woman to have a hijab-wearing Barbie created after her.

Growing up in New Jersey with four siblings, Ibtihaj always had a competitive streak. She loved sports but, having converted to Islam, her parents found that sporting attire often conflicted with their religious beliefs to dress modestly. Many times, Ibtihaj's mum would sew longer sleeves onto tops or cover her daughter's legs. So when they spotted the fencing team practising one night, her mum looked at their trousers and helmets and thought "perfect".

At first, Ibtihaj wasn't sold on fencing. But when she switched her weapon from épée to sabre (considered the fastest and most forceful weapon), she started to excel. And in 2002, Ibtihaj joined the Peter Westbrook Foundation, a non-profit organization that teaches underprivileged young people to fence. She soon became captain of her high school fencing team and secured a scholarship to study International Relations and African-American Studies, with a minor in Arabic, at Duke University. During her time there, she was crowned 2005 Junior Olympic Champion before joining the US national fencing team post-graduation.

Qualifying for the 2016 Rio Olympics was a huge deal – not just for Ibtihaj but also for her family and the Muslim community. She took home an Olympic bronze medal in fencing, which was a massive victory for onlookers across the world.

"A lot of people don't believe that Muslim women have voices or that we participate in sports," Ibtihaj said after competing. "And it's not just to challenge misconceptions outside the Muslim community, but within the Muslim community. I want to break cultural norms."

She has travelled the world speaking about the importance of empowering girls through sport and education. And, noticing a lack of stylish modest fashion in the US, she launched her own clothing company, Louella, along with her brother.

Never one to sit on the fence (sorry!), Ibtihaj has spoken openly about being detained in airports, how she "didn't feel safe" at times growing up in America and some of the ill treatment she received during Olympic training. Every day, she works to break down the barriers she faced and give Muslim women – and all women – a role model they can be proud of.

Ibtihaj 1 – Xenophobia 0. You go, wonder woman.

HER AWESOME ACHIEVEMENTS

→ Became the first Muslim American woman to win an Olympic medal and compete wearing a hijab in 2016.

→ Named Muslim Sportswoman of the Year in 2012.

→ Founded an online shop, Louella, in 2014 specializing in modest and fashionable clothing.

→ Was honoured with her very own Barbie doll in 2017, as part of the brand's programme to celebrate notable women and their achievements.

→ Serves as an ambassador on the US Department of State's Empowering Women and Girls Through Sport initiative.

"I OWE IT TO PEOPLE WHO LOOK LIKE ME. THESE STRUGGLES, THIS EVERYDAY FEAR-MONGERING AND HATE THAT WE ARE EXPERIENCING... I OWE IT TO ALL OF US TO COMBAT THESE THINGS. I HAVE TO SPEAK OUT AGAINST IT BECAUSE THERE WERE PEOPLE BEFORE ME THAT DID."

JANE MATILDA BOLIN

1908–2007

HER SUPERPOWERS:

Yale graduate, policy changer and the US's first black female judge – what a legacy!

HER INCREDIBLE STORY

If you're going to live for nearly 100 years, you might as well leave a lasting impression. And that's exactly what Jane Matilda Bolin did.

Born in 1908 in Poughkeepsie, New York, Jane's family were no strangers to law and order. Her dad, Gaius C. Bolin, was the first black person to graduate from Williams College. He practised law for 50 years and became the first black president of the Dutchess County Bar Association.

The family's intellectual success didn't stop them from facing discrimination. Jane was the daughter of an interracial couple and, in early 1900s America, this meant being refused service in many shops and businesses. It also meant that she wasn't allowed to attend her local college – despite being awesomely intelligent – because they didn't accept black students at the time.

Instead of twiddling her thumbs, Jane enrolled at a college in Massachusetts, where she was one of only two black freshmen. When graduation time approached, a careers advisor tried to discourage her from applying to Yale because of her colour and gender. This didn't stop Jane. She graduated in the top 20 in her class and successfully enrolled at Yale Law School.

In 1931, Jane Matilda Bolin became the first black woman to receive a law degree from Yale and passed the New York State bar exam a year later in 1932. She practised law with her father in Poughkeepsie for a while before joining the New York City Corporation Counsel.

After working as a legal assistant and a brief stint at politics, Jane was called to appear before the Mayor of New York City, Fiorello La Guardia. It was the day that changed her life. Right there and then, he swore her in as the first black female judge in America. Amazing.

As a judge for the Domestic Relations Court, now known as the Family Court, Jane used her platform to instil justice and eradicate inequality. She championed children's services that put children's welfare first, not their ethnic background. Tirelessly, she fought for what was right not what was easy. And it paid off. She changed segregationist policies that had previously been ingrained in the system and helped overturn institutional racism. Her term was renewed three times before she, reluctantly, retired at 70.

Retirement didn't stop Jane from looking after children and women's rights. She volunteered as a school reader and a legal consultant, before passing away in her beloved New York City in 2007.

Breaking down barriers for nearly 100 years, Judge Jane makes the word inspiration seem like an understatement. She might have been a century before our time but she's a timeless reminder not to let anyone else make you feel not good enough or tell you you're not capable – you are.

HER AWESOME ACHIEVEMENTS

➔ Became the first African-American woman to become a judge in 1939.

➔ First African-American woman to graduate from Yale Law School.

➔ Legal advisor to the National Council of Negro Women.

➔ Served on the board of the National Association for the Advancement of Colored People, the National Urban League and the Child Welfare League.

➔ Received honorary degrees from over five different colleges.

"THOSE GAINS WE HAVE MADE WERE NEVER GRACIOUSLY AND GENEROUSLY GRANTED. WE HAVE HAD TO FIGHT EVERY INCH OF THE WAY."

KALPNA WOOLF

DOB UNKNOWN–PRESENT

HER SUPERPOWERS:

The spice-loving wonder woman breaking down stereotypes and bringing cultures together through good food.

HER INCREDIBLE STORY

The uniting power of food. Having worked in food TV production at the BBC for 20 years, Kalpna Woolf set out on a mission of her own: to bring people, cultures and communities together through a shared love of food.

Why? Because often fear of multiculturalism comes from ignorance and a lack of understanding. So, what better way to help combat that than by uniting people from all walks of life together to share amazing food and stories?

It all started with a pop-up International Peace Café in 2015. The multicultural event, hosted by Kalpna Woolf, welcomed people of all ages and backgrounds to enjoy over 120 colourful foods cooked by Iranian, Eritrean, Sudanese and Somalian women from the Refugee Women of Bristol initiative. The wonderful refugee chefs shared memories and stories of their family dishes – leading to empty plates and warmed hearts all round.

It was so well-received that Kalpna then set up 91 Ways to Build a Global Community. The initiative's name is inspired by the fact that there are 91 different languages spoken across communities in Bristol. 91 Ways aims to bridge gaps and build understanding "between groups who may otherwise never meet or move in the same circles". It's a social enterprise initiative that started small but now puts on everything from multi–cultural festivals to more pop-up International Peace Cafés. The aim? To help unite people of different cultures and communities and break down entrenched stereotypes. And what better way to do that than through food?

For Kalpna, food means more than just a bite to eat. It's "a strong symbol of identity". At 91 Ways events, individuals from all walks of life come together to enjoy home-cooked food from different cultures and share stories. The events give refugees and asylum seekers the opportunity to showcase their food and develop their catering skills. A simple idea but a powerful initiative – and one that's helped countless people.

It's refreshing to see a strong, modern woman empowering other strong women from all cultures. Kalpna works tirelessly to bring richness to people's lives and do good in communities near and far. As well as her 91 Ways work, she's a Chair of Trustees for Frank Water – a charity that uses profits from water sales here to provide clean water solutions to save lives in India. She also works closely with centres that help young people get their important first step on the ladder of a media career.

And among her charitable work, cooking and looking after her family, she somehow still finds time to run half marathons and enjoy country walks. Go Kalpna!

HER AWESOME ACHIEVEMENTS

➜ Founded 91 Ways to Build a Global Community to bring cultures and communities together through food.

➜ Wrote *Spice Yourself Slim*, collating her own healthy recipes inspired by cuisines from across the globe.

➜ Won Asian Women of Achievement Award in 2013 in the Media category.

➜ Received an honorary degree from UWE Bristol for her contribution and commitment to economic and social equality and diversity initiatives.

➜ Chair of Trustees for Frank Water charity.

"WE HAVE HEARD STORIES OF LOVE, HAPPINESS, FAMILY, LOSS, WAR, CONFLICT, HEALTH. WHEN PEOPLE GET TOGETHER OVER FOOD, THEY CAN TALK ABOUT ANYTHING."

LAVERNE COX

1984–PRESENT

HER SUPERPOWERS:

LGBTQ advocate, OITNB actress and transgender rights trailblazer – she's one amazing lady.

HER INCREDIBLE STORY

She's the self-confessed "black chick from Alabama" who grew up poor and became one of the most pioneering transgender women in the world.

Childhood wasn't a bed of roses for young Laverne. Home life itself was pleasant; Laverne lived with her twin brother, their mum and grandmother. But school was a time of hardship and hurt, where bullying led to Laverne wanting to commit suicide at just 11. Her teachers were less than sympathetic, so she eventually moved to Alabama School of Fine Arts to study dance – an adventure that "saved her life".

She moved over to New York in her late teens and switched her focus from dancing to acting. Finally away from homophobic bullies, Laverne could be herself and began to identify as gender non-conforming. She landed her first TV gig on *Diddy*, making her the first black trans woman in reality TV – before being cast as Sophia in *Orange is the New Black*. At the time, no one had any idea how successful the Netflix Original show would be so she didn't give up her evening job to start with. In fact, Laverne continued to work nights as a drag queen in Lucky Cheng's bar/restaurant throughout the entire first series.

As the success of *Orange is the New Black* swept the globe, Laverne Cox became a global pioneer. She was the first openly transgender person to be nominated for an Emmy in over 20 years and the first ever to be nominated for a Primetime Emmy Award in acting.

Such awards are just a fraction of her amazing achievements. Laverne is an activist through and through and, as her platform continued to grow, her voice amplified. In 2014, she made history by appearing on the cover of *Time* for "The Transgender Tipping Point" issue. When Caitlyn Jenner unveiled her transition, Laverne wrote a blog congratulating her and also acknowledging "all the trans folk who don't have access to healthcare or embody cisnormative beauty standards".

She's sparked big conversations on important issues that some would shy away from – like the police's treatment of sex workers and the shocking murder statistics of trans women. She's also travelled around America and Canada to share her story and help people understand trans history.

Her work and passion have helped transform how trans people are portrayed in the media and, arguably, the world. But her work isn't done. Laverne continues to be one of the loudest, most important and thoughtful voices in the fight for trans rights. And she makes us very proud to be part of Generation LGBTQ.

HER AWESOME ACHIEVEMENTS

➜ First openly transgender person to be on the cover of *Time* and *Cosmopolitan* magazines.

➜ First openly transgender person to have a waxwork sculpture in Madame Tussauds.

➜ Won an honorary doctorate from The New University for her progressive work in the fight for gender equality.

➜ Won Outstanding Special Class Special as Executive Producer for *Laverne Cox Presents: The T Word* and became the first transgender woman to win a Daytime Emmy.

➜ Made a video about transgender history called "Time Marches Forward & So Do We" in 2017.

"IT IS REVOLUTIONARY FOR ANY TRANS PERSON TO CHOOSE TO BE SEEN AND VISIBLE IN A WORLD THAT TELLS US WE SHOULD NOT EXIST."

LEOMIE ANDERSON

1993–PRESENT

HER SUPERPOWERS:

Castings, catwalks and... cutting-edge activism. Whether she's strutting her way across Victoria's Secret stages or protesting Trump, Leomie Anderson puts the super in supermodel.

HER INCREDIBLE STORY

If you've not heard her name before, you'll have almost certainly seen her face fronting campaigns from Fenty Beauty to Nike and River Island. Leomie Anderson was actually scouted twice as a teen walking home from school in Wimbledon. "So many people told me I should model but I thought it was like when people tell a tall boy he should do sport. I never thought I'd be a face of anything." Today, she's even more than that. She's the voice of something special.

While she's hailed as one of the most successful models around, her career hasn't been without its difficulties. Speaking up about discrimination, Leomie's recounted having to re-do her make-up on toilet seats during fashion weeks – because make-up artists haven't had dark enough foundations – and waiting hours at casting calls only to be turned away as they "don't want any Africans this season".

While we're seeing more models of different colours, shapes and sizes today, Leomie has seen first-hand that darker-skinned models are all too often "treated like second-class citizens" in the industry. Talking about it is the first step but she feels that the only way we're going to truly move forward in the fashion industry is "by having new people, new blood, new ideas and a fresh perspective".

It would be all too easy for a supermodel like Leomie to turn a blind eye, rock up to shoots, bank her fee and post a picture-perfect lifestyle illusion on social media. Instead, she favours "honesty and truth" and demonstrates this in powerful tweets. Why? Because Leomie believes that the fashion industry is "everywhere" and what goes on behind the curtains is arguably just as important as what we see on our glossy magazine pages and TV screens.

She also uses her platform to help females deal with the pressures that today's society brings. Pressures that come in lots of different shapes and sizes. In 2016, her brand LAPP (which stands for "Leomie Anderson the Project the Purpose") launched its first capsule collection focusing on reclaiming boundaries, with slogans such as "This P*ssy Grabs Back". The collection went viral almost immediately – with Rihanna wearing one of their bold hoodies to the 2017 New York Women's March. The brilliant brand also has a booming online presence filled with inspirational blogs and content to provide "a safe space on the internet free from the negativity women face today".

There's a lot we can all learn from this lady, whose dreams are as big as her achievements.

HER AWESOME ACHIEVEMENTS

→ Awesome A level results achieved while modelling (A in English Literature, A in Sociology, B in Media).

→ Walked for Victoria's Secrets Fashion Show. Twice.

→ Rose to fame as part of the Channel 4 series *The Model Agency*.

→ Founded a female empowerment brand at just 23.

→ Walked at Fashion Weeks across the world.

"THE FASHION AND BEAUTY INDUSTRIES NEED TO TAKE A LONG HARD LOOK AND REALIZE THAT THE MARKET ISN'T JUST PALER SKIN TONES."

LORNA SIMPSON

1960–PRESENT

HER SUPERPOWERS:

An incredible artist and photographer whose visions evoke emotions and inspire new perspectives.

HER INCREDIBLE STORY

This queen defines originality. In 2018, she was crowned by *Vogue* as America's "most defiant conceptual artist" – and it all started with a box of tissues.

Flu-stricken one winter, a young Lorna Simpson started cutting out coupons from the back of her Kleenex boxes. It wasn't long before she'd saved up enough for a shiny new Polaroid camera, which she used to take pictures of her beagle-collie.

She lived in New York with her parents at the time. Her mother was a secretary and administrator and her dad was a social worker. They both adored culture and the arts and would often take Lorna to museums, theatre performances and other visual delights. As a result, Lorna was creative from a young age and went on to attend New York's School of Visual Arts as a teen. With her artistic flair, she graduated early with her first degree in Photography and, shortly after, secured an internship at Studio Museum in Harlem.

After finishing her internship, Lorna traded NYC's high-rises for sunnier climes and jetted off to Morocco, Mauritania, Tunisia and Algeria. She took hundreds of documentary-type photos on her travels and started thinking about how few black photographers made it into her art history books and photography lectures. She felt a strong need to redress this and an aspiration to make photography more relevant to modern-day society.

Lorna began to develop her own unique style. She experimented with new creative ways to make people feel through art, bringing important topics – like gender, race, history and identity – to the forefront of her work.

In the early 1980s, Lorna turned traditional photography on its head when she merged photographs of black women with bold text explaining the oppression and injustice that many endure daily. These "photo-text" pieces became her signature style.

Her radically thought-provoking work confronts society's stereotypes of black women both through history and present day. *Guarded Conditions* shows six photos of the same black woman in a plain white dress, standing on a wooden pedestal with her arms folded behind her back. Below, the words "sex attack" and "skin attack" are repeated. It draws visual parallels between historic slave auctions and criminal line-ups of today.

In 1993, Lorna became the first African-American woman to be exhibited at the Venice Biennale. Her work has also wowed in the Tate and the Brooklyn Museum among many other well-respected art venues. Over recent years, she's turned her talented hand to silk-screen printing, painting, video and installation.

Nowadays, she lives a stylish life in Brooklyn with her daughter and her art continues to challenge conventions, inspire minds and paint space for diversity in the fine art world.

HER AWESOME ACHIEVEMENTS

→ Awarded National Endowment for the Arts Fellowship in 1985.

→ Exhibited her work in the most famous locations across the world every year since 1985.

→ First African-American woman to exhibit at Venice Biennale, in 1990.

→ Guest lectures for a range of universities and venues.

→ Won the International Center of Photography's Infinity Award in Art in 2010.

"I FEEL THAT THE YOUNG GENERATION UNDERSTANDS THE HEART OF GENDER AND SEXUALITY CONCEPTS, AND WHERE IT LEADS. I FIND THAT EXCITING AND AMAZING, AND I'M GRATEFUL THAT'S THE CASE."

DR MAE JEMISON

1956–PRESENT

HER SUPERPOWERS:

Doctor, scientist, engineer, astronaut – it's one heck of a resumé. Dr Mae Jemison broke boundaries and shattered stereotypes when she became the first black woman to travel in space.

HER INCREDIBLE STORY

Venturing into space was something Mae had always dreamed of as a young girl growing up in Chicago. She was fascinated by nature, space and stars and spent many happy hours in the school libraries reading about all aspects of science. When asked what she wanted to do by school teachers, Mae proudly replied that she wanted to be a "scientist" – only to be met with puzzled faces and comments such as, "Don't you mean a nurse?" But Mae knew herself. She knew her dream and had been inspired by Martin Luther King's bold talks, thinking of them as "calls to action".

Mae finished high school and went straight to university – at just 16. She graduated with a degree in chemical engineering. It was a time that she enjoyed but studying engineering as a black girl in 1970s America wasn't easy. Mae remembers that some professors would act as if she wasn't there, while others would belittle her sensible questions as if they were the "dumbest questions he'd ever heard". Undeterred, she headed off to Cornell Medical University post-graduation and continued experimenting and exploring. In her time there, she interned at medical centres and jetted off to Cuba, Kenya and Thailand to provide medical care for people there.

Mae worked for the Peace Corps after finishing her studies. There, she provided medical care, researched vaccines and – quite literally – saved lives. She applied for NASA's astronaut program in 1983 and was eventually chosen as one of 15 astronauts out of 2,000 applicants.

After working on launch support activities and computer software challenges, it was mission time for Mae. She flew into space on 12 September 1992 as a Mission Specialist and became the first black woman to enter space. She carried with her some West African art to symbolize that space belongs to everyone, and a picture of Bessie Coleman, the first African-American woman to fly an aeroplane. The first thing she saw from space was her hometown, Chicago.

Mae's dedication to science didn't stop when she left NASA in 1993: she's since lectured at universities, set up her own research company and created a foundation to connect young children with agricultural science. It hasn't always been an easy journey. In 1996, Mae was left hospitalized with a head injury due to a policeman's mistreatment of her over a speeding ticket. She filed a lawsuit against him and didn't let it stop her amazing work – which she's continued on to this day.

HER AWESOME ACHIEVEMENTS

→ Achieved nine honorary degrees from universities across the US.

→ Had five schools and academies named after her – including Mae C. Jemison Space and Science Museum and Mae Jemison Elementary School.

→ Made the International Space Hall of Fame in 2014.

→ Wrote a memoir of her life for children named *Find Where the Wind Goes* in 2001.

→ Founded the Dorothy Jemison Foundation for Excellence, in memory of her mother. It develops and implements teaching methods and materials that help individuals be fully able to contribute effectively to society.

"DON'T LET ANYONE ROB YOU OF YOUR IMAGINATION, YOUR CREATIVITY OR YOUR CURIOSITY. IT'S YOUR PLACE IN THE WORLD AND YOUR LIFE. GO ON AND DO ALL YOU CAN WITH IT."

MALALA YOUSAFZAI

1997–PRESENT

HER SUPERPOWERS:

Shot by the Taliban on a school bus at 15, Nobel Peace Prize winner at 18: the incredible Malala Yousafzai.

HER INCREDIBLE STORY

On 9 October 2012, 15-year-old Malala was making the short bus journey home from school through Swat Valley in Pakistan – an area known for its mountainous valleys, snowy winters and cool summers. She was chatting away to her friend Moniba when she noticed something unfamiliar: silence. The landscape around her was deserted, apart from two men in the distance. They flagged the bus down and jumped on, asking for Malala. Seconds later, she was fighting for her life. Malala had been shot in the head by a Taliban gunman. Her "crime"? Wanting an education.

When girls were banned from education by the Taliban, Malala shared her experience via *The Diary of a Pakistani Schoolgirl* with BBC Urdu under a pseudonym – in a hope that it would help change things for the better. She also bravely interviewed on Pakistani TV about the girls having a right to education. This led to death threats from Taliban militants, who decided to kill her in 2012.

After the shooting, Malala was airlifted to hospital where her condition was diagnosed as life-threatening. The bullet had entered above her brow and travelled down her neck before lodging in her back. Initially, her father feared the worst and told relatives to prepare for the funeral.

Surgery was the only possibility for survival but it was incredibly risky. The part of the brain affected powered speech and limb movement, so there was a risk it could leave her paralyzed. The nation – and world – waited on with hope. The surgery was successful but Malala's post-operative intensive care nearly cost her life, so she was moved to Birmingham, England to be treated by Dr Fiona Reynolds, who had previously assessed her in Pakistan.

Waking up from her coma in a foreign country, Malala communicated only by notebook, which she still has to this day. One of the pages reads "Who did this to me?"

Fast forward nine months of skull reconstruction, physiotherapy and worldwide acclaim, and Malala found herself stood up at the United Nations headquarters, addressing the world on her 16th birthday – just one of many examples of her unimaginable bravery.

After being released from hospital and finishing school in Birmingham, this amazing lady has gone on to study a degree at Oxford. She opened a school for refugees in Syria on her 18th birthday and won a Nobel Peace Prize that same year. She's since written a book, influenced world-leading policy changes and raised billions of dollars for global girls' education rights. And she's only just turned 21.

What a magnificent human. Long live Malala Yousafzai.

HER AWESOME ACHIEVEMENTS

➔ Achieved six As and four A*s at GCSE just three years after being shot.

➔ Became the youngest person ever to win a Nobel Peace Prize in 2015.

➔ Founded the Malala Fund, which received its first donation of $200,000 from Angelina Jolie and helped secure $2.7 billion in donations for girls' education in 2017.

➔ Led the first ever Youth Takeover of the UN on "Malala Day", her 16th birthday.

➔ After the shooting, 2 million people signed the Right to Education petition, which led to the first Right to Education Bill being passed in Pakistan.

"I DON'T WANT TO BE REMEMBERED AS THE GIRL WHO WAS SHOT, I WANT TO BE REMEMBERED AS THE GIRL WHO STOOD UP."

MALORIE BLACKMAN

1962–PRESENT

HER SUPERPOWERS:

This award-winning writer's imaginative mind portrayed race like never before in a story of love, growing up and inequality.

HER INCREDIBLE STORY

Malorie Blackman always loved children's books. As a shy young girl with a passion for the subject of English Literature, she looked up at her teacher and confessed that she'd like to follow in her footsteps when she was older. Her response? A pitying look and a comment that Malorie will never forget: "Black people don't become teachers, they become secretaries."

It knocked her confidence and Malorie parked her teaching dreams and went on to study Computer Sciences, working in programming for years. She didn't hate the job but itchy feet crept in after nine years and she longed for something more creative.

Then came the lightbulb moment. At 23, Malorie was wandering round a bookstore when she stumbled across *The Color Purple*. It was the first book she'd ever seen that featured characters that looked like her. A book featuring black people, written by a black women. For some, it might mean nothing but for Malorie, it meant everything. It was hope.

From that moment on, she wrote. She wrote short stories, long stories, picture stories. She sent them off to publishers and, as the rejection letters piled up, she carried on. Eighty-six rejections later, she finally got her well-deserved break. An editor agreed to publish her first book, *Not So Stupid* – the first chapter in her amazing novelist story.

She left her job in computing and became a full-time writer (in your face, mean teacher). But only after 49 books and 12 years was she ready to tackle a topic close to her heart – racism.

Noughts and Crosses focuses on race in a brilliantly thought-provoking way. It's set in a dystopian universe where darker-skinned people, Crosses, are the dominant race and hold the power, politics and prestige. White people, Noughts, are marginalized and live a very different life. Cue Nought children forced to use glaring brown plasters as products are manufactured around Crosses. The hard-to-put-down novel follows a young Nought and Cross down their path of forbidden romance.

The book picked up award after award and the Noughts and Crosses series has sold nearly two million copies worldwide. In 2013, Malorie followed in Quentin Blake and Jacqueline Wilson's footsteps to become the Children's Laureate – the national figure in charge of promoting children's interest in literature and reading in the United Kingdom. Since then, she's fought to keep libraries open, spoken out about big issues and still found time to write more books! It's safe to say that she proved that teacher epically wrong. In fact, a Brexit-inspired fifth book in the Noughts and Crosses series is in progress. Yes, yes and more yes.

HER AWESOME ACHIEVEMENTS

→ Appointed OBE in the 2008 Queen's Birthday Honours.

→ Appointed Children's Laureate from 2013 to 2015.

→ Co-wrote the "Rosa" episode of Doctor Who in 2018, one of the most talked-about in the 11th series.

→ Won over 15 awards for her amazing work over the years.

→ Topped Powerful Media's Powerlist of influential black people.

→ Supported the Let Books Be campaign, which seeks to stop books being labelled "for boys" or "for girls".

"MY VIEW IS TO TAKE PEOPLE AS THEMSELVES. I DON'T BELIEVE IN LIVING LIFE IN HATRED AND ANGER. LIFE'S TOO SHORT."

MARY MAHONEY

1845–1926

HER SUPERPOWERS:

She dreamed of racial equality and became the first African-American woman to register as a nurse. A loving legend.

HER INCREDIBLE STORY

Mary Elizabeth Mahoney was born in Massachusetts. Her parents were free slaves who fled from North Carolina in search of a life with less racial discrimination. They had four children of whom Mary was the eldest. One of her siblings died at a young age – perhaps sparking her passion to help people.

At 10, Mary joined one of the first integrated schools in Boston. This opened a whole new world for her and she learned about everything from morality to maths. She knew from then that she wanted to be a nurse, although it was a profession not pursued by black women at the time.

To gain experience, Mary started working at the New England Hospital for Women and Children as a cook, janitor and washer woman. She worked there for 15 years before starting a 16-month nursing programme in 1878. It was advertised for "well and strong applicants, between the ages of 21 and 31" but Mary was accepted on the programme despite being 33. For a year, she worked from 5.30 a.m. to 9.30 p.m. learning vital skills and bedside manner, and going to lectures and lessons in between.

It paid off and Mary graduated in 1879. She was one of just four successful colleagues out of 47. She made history by becoming the first black woman to become a registered nurse in the US.

After graduating, Mary decided against public nursing because of mass discrimination at the time.

Instead, she became a private care nurse, working mostly for wealthy families. She hoped to change the way people thought of minority nurses and abolish discrimination in nursing – two things that she definitely helped to do. She quickly built up an impeccable reputation for her bedside manner and efficiency and started receiving lots of private nursing requests.

In 1896, Mary joined the Nurses Associated Alumnae of the United States and Canada (NAAUSC). She found the association unwelcoming of African-American women, so she set up the National Association of Colored Graduate Nurses (NACGN) with 51 other African-American nurses. Together, the group celebrated the accomplishments of all outstanding nurses and didn't discriminate against anyone. Mary received lifetime membership for her amazing work. She also became Director of the Howard Orphan Asylum – a home for freed children and the elderly – around the same time. There she did what she did best: looking after people in need of support.

After a long and brilliant career, Mary retired but never stopped caring about equality. She championed civil rights and, when women's suffrage was achieved, she was one of the first to register to vote in Boston. Mary passed away three years later, but her kind legacy lives on to this day.

HER AWESOME ACHIEVEMENTS

→ Became the first African-American to graduate as a registered nurse in 1879.

→ Co-founded the National Association of Colored Graduate Nurses in 1908.

→ Mary E. Mahoney Medal celebrates outstanding examples of nursing to this day.

→ Named in the Nursing Hall of Fame in 1976 and National Woman's Hall of Fame in 1993.

→ Honoured by US Congress in April 2006.

DR MAYA ANGELOU

1928–2014

HER SUPERPOWERS:

*Poet, storyteller, activist, dancer, director, civil rights
leader, survivor. An inspiration – and then some.*

HER INCREDIBLE STORY

Maya Angelou. The name behind some of Instagram's most #empowering quotes. But did you know that it was five years of being mute that developed her world-inspiring love for language?

Born in 1928 in Missouri, Marguerite "Maya" Angelou's childhood was far from easy. At just eight years old, she was raped by her mother's boyfriend. When Maya found the courage to speak out about this, her rapist was murdered by her uncles for his crime. It was this harrowing experience that led to Maya becoming mute. Convinced her "voice was so powerful it could kill people" she didn't speak to anyone but her beloved brother, Bailey, for almost half a decade.

Her lack of verbal communication didn't stop her love of language – far from it. Maya read continuously during her chapter of silence. And when she was 12, an educated black woman, Mrs Flowers (later chronicled in *Mrs Flowers: A Moment of Friendship*) helped Maya find her voice again.

Surviving a traumatic childhood was just the start of Maya's magnificent accomplishments in life. At 16, she broke history by becoming San Francisco's first black and first female cable car conductor before later giving birth to her son, Guy – all while studying at California Labor School.

During Guy's early life, she took on a number of jobs – ranging from hamburger chef to calypso dancer.

But it wasn't long before she exchanged her dancing shoes for pen and paper and rekindled her love affair with the written word. She joined the Harlem Writers Guild and, shortly after, met Martin Luther King. He became a close friend and a catalyst for her civil rights activism. She worked closely with him, devoting her time to fighting against inequality and oppression. But darkness descended again for Maya when Martin Luther King was shot on her birthday in 1968. She stopped celebrating her birthdays for years but battled for justice for the rest of her life.

Encouraged by a good friend, Maya channelled her experiences and emotions into her first book, *I Know Why the Caged Bird Sings*. To this day, it's known as one of the most influential autobiographies of all time.

Finding the bravery to document her struggles and survival paved the foundation for Maya's legacy of inspiration. She went on to write six more autobiographies, inaugurate a president, earn a doctorate and she never stopped fighting for freedom. In fact, she was awarded the Presidential Medal for Freedom by Barack Obama just four years before she died.

Her most powerful qualities? Hope and courage. Maya never gave up. She bounced back. In her very own words: "You may encounter many defeats but you must never be defeated." She's an inspiration to all who've struggled.

HER AWESOME ACHIEVEMENTS

→ Organized key events during the Civil Rights Movement, along with Martin Luther King and Malcolm X.

→ The first female poet to recite a poem for a US presidential inauguration.

→ The first black woman to write a screenplay for a major film release (*Georgia, Georgia*, 1972).

→ Received the Presidential Medal of Freedom, the highest civil honour in the US, from Obama.

→ Awarded honorary degrees from more than 50 universities.

"I'VE LEARNED THAT PEOPLE WILL FORGET WHAT YOU SAID, PEOPLE WILL FORGET WHAT YOU DID, BUT PEOPLE WILL NEVER FORGET HOW YOU MADE THEM FEEL."

MICHELLE OBAMA

1969–PRESENT

HER SUPERPOWERS:

Lawyer, mother, global education programme creator and more. She's the First Lady who changed the game, with beliefs as on point as her outfits.

HER INCREDIBLE STORY

Obama. It's a name that few were familiar with until a decade ago. And America's former president Barack Obama is only half responsible for this surname's fame. He didn't break history alone; he did it hand-in-hand with the First Lady of all First Ladies. Loved for more than just her colourful two-pieces and class, Michelle Obama somehow made the pressures of the presidential spotlight look effortless.

It started back in 1989, when Michelle was assigned as Barack's mentor at the law firm she worked at. It wasn't quite love at first sight. Despite all his "smooth talking" Michelle initially turned Barack down, thinking that dating him in the workplace would be "tacky". She eventually agreed to go on a cinema date, where they bumped into his professor at the popcorn stand (awkward). It was the start of something special. Things blossomed from there and they were married three years later.

In 2006, they were living in Chicago with their two young daughters. Michelle was working as Executive Director of Community Affairs at University of Chicago Hospitals and her husband as a senator. She'd made an agreement with him that she'd support his political ambitions only if he gave up smoking. He kicked the habit and Michelle started on his 2008 presidential campaign. She became known for writing her own speeches and reciting them powerfully without notes.

Her support paid off then – and again in 2012. Strong and smart, Michelle did much more than shake hands and smile politely. She made change happen. She brought political leaders to her house to explain why women's rights were critical. She worked with Barack to repeal the law against gay or bisexual people serving in the military, and she passed a programme to give free or reduced-price lunches to 21 million low-income children. What's more, she introduced the initiative Let Girls Learn to educate and empower young women. And she didn't stop with America; she went global. In less than a decade this wonder woman raised over $3.5 billion to give young girls a fair education around the world.

While her White House days are no longer, her brilliant work is ongoing. She's hand-delivered countless talks encouraging girls to be the change they want to see in the world. For someone who "never had a passion for politics", Michelle Obama has done an outstanding job of reinvigorating hope, fairness and empathy in democracy – all while being a mum, a role model and one heck of a style icon.

The only sad news is that she doesn't fancy running for president herself. Cry.

HER AWESOME ACHIEVEMENTS

→ The first black First Lady of the USA.

→ Fundraised record amounts as Executive Director for the Chicago office of Public Allies, a non-profit organization encouraging young people to work on social issues.

→ Raised and contributed over $3 billion to launch education programmes for young girls across the world.

→ Her daughter is following in her intellectual footsteps and studying at Harvard.

→ The only First Lady to ever rap with Missy Elliot, while driving around the Oval grounds doing Carpool Karaoke. Enough said.

"YOU SEE, WHILE OUR MOTHERS AND GRANDMOTHERS WERE OFTEN POWERLESS TO CHANGE THEIR CIRCUMSTANCES, TODAY, WE AS WOMEN HAVE ALL THE POWER WE NEED TO DETERMINE THE OUTCOME OF THIS ELECTION. WE HAVE KNOWLEDGE. WE HAVE A VOICE."

NICOLA ADAMS OBE

1982–PRESENT

HER SUPERPOWERS:

36 years old, 1.6 m (5 ft 4 in) tall and officially the most successful female boxer of all time. Enter the one and only Nicola Adams.

HER INCREDIBLE STORY

The first female boxer to represent England and the first woman to win Olympic gold for boxing, Nicola Adams is the personification of tenacity, and her success is far from coincidental. "I never go to a tournament thinking I'll be happy with just a medal. I'm only happy with gold."

Nicola was raised by her mum for most of her childhood and attributes her boxing success to her strength. Growing up, things weren't always easy. Her father was abusive to the point that Nicola remembers jumping in front of her mum to try and separate them. She begged her mum to leave and, eventually, she did. With two kids to provide for, her mum worked two jobs day and night. It taught Nicola that "if you work hard, you can achieve anything you want to."

Nicola started boxing a couple of years after her father left. Her matches got bigger and bigger and she became well known for her sparring talents. She trained tirelessly – but things took a catastrophic turn in 2009. Nicola was on her way to an important bout when she slipped on a boxing bandage and fell down the stairs. Nicola, being Nicola, didn't stay down for long – she picked herself up and headed to the fight. Somehow she won the match but, in doing so, she seriously damaged her back and spent the next year out of the ring. She spent months in recovery, living penniless at her mum's house, unable to lift a glass of milk let alone a boxing glove.

To make matters worse, Nicola's dream of women's boxing being introduced to the Olympics came true while she was out of action. She was devastated and, when the Team GB squad selection trials came round, she refused to miss out. She got up and fought and, despite being severely injured, convinced the panel that she'd be squad-ready for the Olympics.

Her recovery journey was gruelling. She'd gone from being able to do 300 sit-ups a day to one. But in 2012, it all paid off. At the 2012 London Olympics, Nicola Adams overcame pain and odds to become the first ever woman to win an Olympic boxing gold. She defended the title four years later, becoming the first British boxer to hold on to an Olympic title in nearly a century.

Incredible, right? But what's her secret? What keeps a record-breaking boxing champion focused? Chess, apparently. Who'd have thought it?

HER AWESOME ACHIEVEMENTS

➜ First female boxer to win an Olympic gold.

➜ First British boxer to successfully defend an Olympic title since 1924.

➜ Received an MBE and OBE for outstanding services to boxing.

➜ Awarded the MOBO Paving the Way Award in 2016.

➜ First female boxer to receive an award from the Boxing Writers' Club.

"WOMAN BOXERS HAVE COME A LONG WAY. IN THE 90S, YOU ONLY EVER SAW WOMEN PARADING AROUND IN HEELS AND A BIKINI HOLDING A SCORECARD. NOW WE'RE OWNING IT, WE SHOULD GET SOME MALE MODELS IN SPEEDOS TO DO THE RING WALK."

NIKITA GILL

1987–PRESENT

HER SUPERPOWERS:

Poetry meets girl power. From beautiful books to uplifting insta-posts, Nikita Gill's words have soul-soothing magic powers like no other.

HER INCREDIBLE STORY

Ah, classic fairy tales. You know the sort: hero overcomes villain, saves helpless girl, plants a kiss on her and they saunter happily off into the sunset.

But when you look at them through a different lens:

Who ruled that princesses can't be powerful? Or that damsels should have to wait in distress? What if happy endings didn't require being rescued by a prince? Or snogging pondlife in the desperate hope of becoming a wife?

Nikita Gill is tackling exactly that. She's changing the face of traditional tales, one page at a time.

Nikita has been writing from the heart for over a decade. Today, her work fills books and heals the hearts of some half a million insta-followers. But her storytelling journey has gone through many stages. Nikita was born in Belfast and moved to New Delhi, India, at just a few months old. At school, she was a self-confessed "naughty kid" who didn't care much for homework. One of her teachers saw beyond this and noticed her creative brilliance, which gave Nikita the encouragement to put pen to paper.

She rose to modest fame at just 12 years old when a story she wrote about her grandad as a young man was published in a local newspaper. That feeling of sharing, not just telling, stories stuck with her.

Over her young adult years, Nikita went through some traumatic experiences. She endured bullying and abusive relationships and grew sick of men in New Delhi undressing her with their eyes. She channelled some of her anger back into her writing as a way of "coping with the world". It became cathartic – a feeling she wanted to share with others. Nikita started posting to a Tumblr blog and sending out manuscripts to publishing companies. It wasn't long before the two worlds collided. An editor saw one of her collections online and asked if she'd be interested in having a book published.

Four incredible books, countless topics and a colossal fan base later, her words are just as magical as ever. Nikita Gill is redefining poetry for the modern day. She uses Instagram as a platform for her heart-warming poems, which are shared by millions across the world. There's a realness and relatability to everything she writes – whether it's a hundred word insta-poem about heartbreak and hope or one of her hugely popular books.

She's known as an Instagram sensation but there's a lot more to this queen than followers and filters. She speaks honestly to women of all ages about self-kindness, shunning beauty stereotypes and loving yourself. And in an era when social media can feel all about looks and likes, we need more amazing lionesses like Gill.

HER AWESOME ACHIEVEMENTS

→ Published four books in less than three years: *Your Soul is a River*, *Wild Embers*, *Disconnected* and *Fierce Fairytales.*

→ Also creates visuals and illustrations to go alongside many of her poems and stories.

→ Writes regular articles for Thought Catalog, helping people heal, deal with difficulties and grow to love themselves.

→ Worked as a carer and teaching assistant for young people with disabilities before starting to publish her work.

→ Has a Master's degree in Book Arts and Publishing.

"DEFINED BY NO MAN, YOU ARE YOUR OWN STORY, BLAZING THROUGH THE WORLD, TURNING HISTORY INTO HERSTORY."

NINA SIMONE

1933–2003

HER SUPERPOWERS:

A pianist, an activist and a unique voice that's been putting a spell on all of us for decades – the unforgettable Nina Simone.

HER INCREDIBLE STORY

Born Eunice Waymon, Nina loved music from a young age. She landed her first gig at 12. It was a classical recital and, naturally, her parents sat proudly in the front row. Before she started, Nina looked out into the audience and was horrified to see her mum and dad being forced out of their seats to make room for a white couple. She got up from her piano and refused to play until they were given their rightful spaces.

Sadly, this wasn't the last time Nina experienced racial injustice. After graduating from high school, she spent the whole summer studying for an audition at the Curtis Institute of Music in Philadelphia – only for her application to be denied without explanation. It was a big blow, especially as her family had moved there so she could pursue her dream. Instead, Nina took a job as a photographer's assistant to pay for private lessons with one of the institute's teachers, and eventually began giving lessons herself.

In 1954, she started playing piano at a Midtown bar to earn cash to pay for her private lessons. The owner insisted that she sing as well as play and, knowing that her mother wouldn't approve of her singing "the devil's music", she adopted the stage name Simone (after one of her favourite actresses, Simone Signoret).

Her rise to stardom was almost accidental. The song "I Loves You, Porgy", a cover of a song from the musical *Porgy and Bess*, was recorded as a favour for a friend and became a top 20 hit. Soon after, she signed a contract with Colpix Records. For Nina, pop music was just something she did to fund her classical music studies.

In the late 1960s, she became a key figure in the rising civil rights movement. She wrote "Mississippi Goddam" in response to the KKK Birmingham Church bombing that killed four young black girls and partially blinded another. She also called out the Jim Crow laws that drove segregation and sung about the Eurocentric beauty standards placed on black women. Her racial activism wasn't always welcomed. As she sung out about matters close to her heart, like oppression and feminism, certain venues stopped inviting her to perform and some radio stations stopped playing her songs. Of course, this didn't stop Queen Nina. In fact, she spoke out more.

Nina Simone was an activist and artist who influenced thousands with her powerful lyrics and sound. She lived a life that was as fascinating as her musical talent before passing away in 2003. And for someone nonplussed by pop music, she's certainly left a lasting impression on this world.

HER AWESOME ACHIEVEMENTS

→ Named one of the greatest singers of all time by *Rolling Stone*, who said "her honey-coated, slightly adenoidal cry was one of the most affecting voices of the civil rights movement".

→ Wrote her autobiography, *I Put a Spell on You*, with Stephen Cleary in 1992.

→ Two days before her death, she learned that she would be awarded an honorary degree by the Curtis Institute of Music – the school that refused her entry at the beginning of her career.

→ Inducted into the Rock and Roll Hall of Fame in 2018, by Mary J. Blige.

→ Earned the title Highest Priestess of Soul (after one of her own albums) for her stage presence and ability to play the piano, sing and perform "both simultaneously and separately".

"WHAT KEPT ME SANE WAS KNOWING THAT THINGS WOULD CHANGE, AND IT WAS A QUESTION OF KEEPING MYSELF TOGETHER UNTIL THEY DID."

OPRAH WINFREY

1954–PRESENT

HER SUPERPOWERS:

She's moonwalked with MJ, campaigned with the Obamas and hosted some of the world's most famous faces. She's a super-generous philanthropist too. What's not to love about Queen O?

HER INCREDIBLE STORY

There is no other story like Oprah's. This wonder lady runs an entire TV network, has her own magazine (with her face on the cover every week) and still finds time to act, write and inspire a generation.

It wasn't a starry start for Oprah, though. She was born to a poor family in rural Mississippi. Her life took a horrific turn when she was raped by her cousin at just nine, while she babysat. The harrowing sexual abuse continued, by numerous perpetrators, long into her teenage years and she fell pregnant at 14. She was so petrified she contemplated suicide. The baby was born prematurely and died two weeks after birth.

Shortly after, Oprah was kicked out by her mother and, with nowhere to go, moved in with her father. It was a turning point in her life. Her father encouraged her to focus on education and she did a lot more than just that: she excelled at it.

Oprah found her passion in drama and public speaking and won a scholarship to a local university. She was crowned Miss Black Tennessee and landed a job at a local radio station the same year – all at just 17. She became a well-known voice on the radio and when she was offered the role of news anchor for a local TV channel, Oprah dropped out of university with her final paper left to complete.

Oprah spent the following years anchoring in a TV industry then dominated by white males. She took over a low-rating Chicago breakfast show in 1984. In just a few months, she'd turned it around and it was ranked top of the charts. Oprah was such a popular host that two years later the show was renamed *The Oprah Winfrey Show*. The same year, she went back to university to finish her final paper and graduate.

The Oprah Winfrey Show became the biggest chat show of all times. Barack Obama, Michael Jackson and Elizabeth Taylor were all welcomed onto her sofa. Mixing celebrities with reality, she also covered big topics like interracial relationships, coming out and performance-enhancing drugs.

The final *Oprah* was aired (with watery eyes) in 2011. But her awe-inspiring work hasn't faltered. Much more than just the "Queen of Media", Oprah is a reigning queen of philanthropy and has donated over $500 million to educational and charitable causes in recent years, including $500,000 to gun violence survivors and $40 million to create a school for hundreds of girls in a poverty-stricken part of South Africa (who she teaches via satellite).

The media call her one of the world's most powerful women. But there are few savvier business people or greater philanthropists around than this one. An incredible human, who deserves every last second of her success.

HER AWESOME ACHIEVEMENTS

→ Became the first black person to rank in the 50 Most Generous Americans in 2004.

→ Played the role of Sofia in the 1985 movie version of *The Color Purple*.

→ Her 1993 interview with Michael Jackson became the most watched interview ever.

→ Her endorsement of Obama is believed to have brought in over a million votes to his 2008 election.

→ Her charity, Oprah's Angel Network, raised more than $80 million to support charitable projects and provide grants to non-profit organizations around the world.

"BE THANKFUL FOR WHAT YOU HAVE; YOU'LL END UP HAVING MORE. IF YOU CONCENTRATE ON WHAT YOU DON'T HAVE, YOU WILL NEVER, EVER HAVE ENOUGH."

PHILOMENA KWAO

1990–PRESENT

HER SUPERPOWERS:

One shade doesn't fit all, and this self-confessed economics geek and stunning model is taking the plus-size industry by storm.

HER INCREDIBLE STORY

Remember when size 0 was the term on everyone's lips and size 10 was deemed "too big" for a model? Well, it's thanks to beauties like Philomena Kwao that those days are fast changing.

Since winning a nationwide modelling contest for Evans, London-born Philomena Kwao has been turning heads on billboards and big screens. Her beautiful dark skin and size 16 curves are a far cry from the early noughties school of modelling. But, from early in her career, one of Philomena's missions was to "help spread the message that there is beauty in every size, shape, height and colour". High five to that, queen.

Her striking looks go hand-in-hand with her super-smart mind. Philomena is a self-confessed "economics geek" with not one but two degrees – a first-class undergraduate degree in Economics and a Masters in International Health Management. Her studies made her think deeply about health and ways that we can better provide access to healthcare across the world. This is something that she advocates actively as global ambassador for the Women for Women International charity.

Amid contracts and campaigns with the likes of MAC, Nordstrom and *Cosmopolitan*, Philomena dedicates time to inspiring the next generations. She's written a children's book called *The Queen in Me*, which celebrates Afrocentric features and aims to change the golden-locked portrayal of fairytale beauty. She has her own charity too, The Lily Project. It's an open forum where young girls can ask personal questions and receive supportive responses from mentors.

Philomena speaks and writes openly about the complex issues of identity, nationality and colourism, reminding the world that there's no one-shade-fits-all when it comes to being black or African. She's shared her own experiences and discussed how she struggled to get modelling work when she first moved to New York, as many jobs would opt for lighter-skinned black models with more of a "girl next door" look. Thankfully, those days have subsided and Kwao's career has flourished. Highlights include modelling in the #SwimSexy outcry against Protein World's Beach Body Ready campaign and shoots for *Galore* magazine where she's absolutely rocking traditional Ghanaian headdresses.

In just a matter of years, Philomena Kwao has played a key part in redefining the industry standard of beauty (and has somehow found time to speak out, study hard and get married along the way). She doesn't plan on putting her feet up anytime soon either. She'll be continuing to model but would ultimately like to use her voice to "advance healthcare access around the world".

We have no doubt this won't be the last we hear about this wonder woman.

HER AWESOME ACHIEVEMENTS

→ Global Ambassador for Women for Women International.

→ Author of *The Queen in Me* children's book.

→ Starred in Lane Bryant's #TheNewSkinny campaign to redefine model beauty.

→ A first-class degree in Economics from University of Bristol and a Masters in International Health Management from Imperial College, London.

→ Founder of The Lily Project charity.

"BEAUTY FOR ME MEANS CONFIDENCE AND COMPLETE COMFORT IN YOURSELF, DISREGARDING WHATEVER ANYONE SAYS TO YOU OR WHAT SOCIETY SAYS YOU SHOULD BE."

ROBYN "RIHANNA" FENTY

1988–PRESENT

HER SUPERPOWERS:

She can sing. She can dance. She's stunningly beautiful and she's achieved more in her three decades than you could shake an umbrella at. But there's a whole lot more to Ri-Ri than just unforgettable bangers and being able to werk, werk, werk it.

HER INCREDIBLE STORY

Flash back to the 1990s and Robyn "Rihanna" Fenty was selling clothes with her dad on the streets of Saint Michael in Barbados. She lived in a three-bedroom bungalow with her mum, Monica (a retired accountant), her dad, Ronald (a warehouse supervisor) and her two brothers, Rorry and Rajad. It's fair to say that home life wasn't the easiest back then. Her father was battling a crack cocaine addiction and Rihanna was suffering from crippling headaches that were so bad that doctors thought they could be due to a tumour.

When her parents divorced at 14, her health started to improve – along with her confidence – and at 15, she formed a girl band with two schoolmates. They were invited to audition for big-time music producer Evan Rogers on his visit to Barbados. Rogers was blown away by Rihanna, admitting that "the minute she walked into the room, it was like the other two girls didn't exist".

Despite Rihanna having no formal vocal or dance training, Rogers whisked her off to America to work on her demo (promising her mother that he wouldn't let her forget about her education). Shortly after, in 2004, she recorded "Pon De Replay" – the hit that changed her life. Her demo was sent out to numerous labels and when it landed at Jay-Z's desk, he invited Rihanna to audition. CEO of the label, L. A. Reid, heard Rihanna sing and told Jay-Z not to let her leave the building without signing the contract.

The rest is history – and what an incredible one it's been. Beautiful, bold and brave, Rihanna has overcome some painful struggles and super successes on her journey to being one of the world's biggest superstars. She's had 13 singles reach number one – the same number as Michael Jackson. She's racked up more awards in a decade than most stars in a lifetime. She's walked catwalks, dazzled carnivals and reinvented clothing lines. And, most amazingly, she's used her platform to give back and do good. The Clara Lionel Foundation, founded in memory of her grandparents, has raised over $5 million to give impoverished communities the right to health and education.

She's an entrepreneurial game-changer too. Her beauty and underwear lines were created with the vision of "inclusion for all women" and Rihanna hand-selects real women of all beautiful shades and sizes to showcase both brands. Her vision is paying off for all the right reasons: Fenty Beauty was crowned one of *Time*'s best inventions of 2017 alongside NASA's Martian spacecraft, InSight.

From Brits to BETs and Grammys to Guinness World Records, Rihanna has bagged them all, and at an age much younger than most. So, cheers to Ri-Ri – and to a future as diamond bright as her story so far. We'll drink to that.

HER AWESOME ACHIEVEMENTS

➔ Made *Guinness World Records* for most US No. 1 singles in a year and most consecutive weeks on UK singles chart.

➔ Founded the Clara Lionel Foundation in memory of her grandparents. It aims to improve the quality of life for communities in need across the world.

➔ Has had the third most number one hits of all time.

➔ Donated $100,000 to the Hurricane Sandy relief effort in 2012.

➔ Named Harvard University's "Humanitarian of the Year" in 2017.

➔ Creator of a multi-award-winning beauty line dedicated to "inclusivity" and providing make-up options for people of all colours.

"I ALWAYS BELIEVED THAT WHEN YOU FOLLOW YOUR HEART OR YOUR GUT, WHEN YOU REALLY FOLLOW THE THINGS THAT FEEL GREAT TO YOU, YOU CAN NEVER LOSE. BECAUSE SETTLING IS THE WORST FEELING IN THE WORLD."

ROBYN "RIHANNA" FENTY

ROSA PARKS

1913–2005

HER SUPERPOWERS:

One small word, one huge impact. When Rosa Parks said "no", she made a stand that changed people's lives around the world – and she'll forever be remembered for it.

HER INCREDIBLE STORY

It was around 6 p.m. on a fairly cool December evening. Rosa Parks was waiting for the bus home, after working all day as a seamstress in an Alabama department store. She was looking forward to having dinner with her husband and taking the weight off her feet.

When the bus arrived, Rosa got on and sat in the middle section. The front of the bus was reserved for white people and the back was for black people. The middle, where Rosa sat, was unreserved and operated on a "first come, first served" basis, although black passengers were expected to give up their seats for whites if white people were standing. A few stops later, the driver noticed the bus was full and told Rosa and three other black people to move from the middle and let white passengers sit down.

It was then that this unremarkable Alabama evening became very, very different. It was that very moment that changed history.

After decades of segregation and verbal and physical abuse because of the colour of her skin, Rosa had had enough. She was tired – not just from work – but from a life of oppression. So when the driver told her for a second time to give up her seat, she said "No" and calmly but correctly told him that she'd paid the same fare, gotten on board first and wasn't sitting in the dedicated white section. He told her that if she didn't give up the seat, he'd have her arrested to which she replied "You may do that."

Rosa was arrested and fined $14 but what happened next changed the lives of people across the state, the country and the world.

Word spread quickly about Rosa's arrest and four days later, the Montgomery Bus Boycott began: over 40,000 black people across Alabama refused to ride buses in protest against segregated seating. Inspired by Rosa's civil rights action and championed by Martin Luther King, it was the first large-scale protest against segregation in the US and the beginning of the American civil rights movement.

During the boycott, African-American taxi drivers reduced their fares to 10 cents to help those boycotting get around. Other boycotters walked 20 miles to work every day. The boycott lasted 381 days, and ended only when Montgomery stopped segregated seating following a court ruling that segregation on public transportation was against the law.

It's important to remember that this wasn't just an isolated incident for Rosa. She had lived through inequality her entire life. Her brave decision to finally say "no" echoed through America, giving people hope and the motivation to stand against inequality. She received countless accolades for her inspirational act, from the prestigious Martin Luther King Award to the Presidential Medal of Freedom. Gone but never forgotten, her legacy is a reminder that one small act really can change the world.

HER AWESOME ACHIEVEMENTS

→ Awarded Martin Luther King Jr. Award by NAACP in 1992.

→ Awarded State of Alabama's Governor's Medal of Honor for Extraordinary Courage in 2000.

→ Awarded the Peace Abbey Courage of Conscience Award for her years dedicated to social change through non-violent means in 1992.

→ Presented Presidential Medal of Freedom (highest honour a civilian can receive from US Government) in 1996.

→ Named one of "The Most Influential Figures of 20th Century" by *Time* magazine in 1999.

"I BELIEVE WE ARE HERE ON THE PLANET EARTH TO LIVE, GROW UP AND DO WHAT WE CAN TO MAKE THIS WORLD A BETTER PLACE FOR ALL TO ENJOY FREEDOM."

RUBY BRIDGES

1954–PRESENT

HER SUPERPOWERS:

She took down segregation in schools at just six years old – and she's been doing amazing things for civil rights ever since.

HER INCREDIBLE STORY

First days at school can be terrifying at the best of times. But imagine being the first black person to set foot in an all-white school at just six years old.

Holding her mother's hand and surrounded by US marshals, young Ruby Bridges walked up the stairs to start her very first day at William Frantz Elementary School, New Orleans, in 1960. Crowds of protestors had gathered to throw things and shout death threats at the little girl. Why? Because she was black.

Six years earlier, the courts had ruled for schools to be desegregated rather than divided by skin colour as they previously had been. But some southern states, like Louisiana, had been reluctant to change. Even when the government started to pressure them, schools in the area introduced entrance exams designed to try and keep black children out. Ruby Bridges was one of just six black children to pass. Her dad was worried about her going to a mixed school, given the civil unrest, but her mum saw it as an opportunity for Ruby to have a better education. Why should she be held back?

Dressed beautifully in her new school attire (cute little bow and all), young Ruby walked so bravely through the angry crowds that even the US marshals accompanying her were proud. "She showed a lot of courage. She just marched along like a little solider and we're all very, very proud of her."

Her first year at school was far from perfect. It was chaos, in fact. Lots of parents withdrew their children from the school and only one teacher, Barbara Henry, was happy to teach Ruby. Miss Henry taught Ruby for a whole year alone "as if she were teaching a whole class" and became her only confidante and friend. Every day for months, Ruby would walk up to the school only to be taunted by black baby dolls in coffins and parents threatening to poison her food. It affected the whole family. Her dad was dismissed from his job as a gas station attendant. The grocery shop stopped letting them shop there and Ruby's grandparents were turned off their land. Kinder members of the community, however, would walk behind the US marshals' car in support as she left, watch Ruby's house in protection and look out for the family's welfare.

Unsurprisingly, Ruby became a symbolic character in the civil rights movement – and continued her involvement into her adult life. Today, she chairs The Ruby Bridges Foundation, which focuses on the "values of toleration, respect and appreciation of all differences".

And for someone who went through so much so young, she's remained brave, strong and full of light to this day. A civil rights icon and a truly beautiful human.

HER AWESOME ACHIEVEMENTS

➜ The first student to attend an all-white school in New Orleans in 1960.

➜ Received the Presidential Citizens Medal in 2001.

➜ Her story was told in a TV movie called *Ruby's Story* in 2005.

➜ Honoured in the Anti-Defamation League's Concert Against Hate in 2006.

➜ Met Barack Obama in 2011 and while looking together at Norman Rockwell's famous portrait of young Ruby, Obama said "I think it's fair to say that if it wasn't for you guys, I wouldn't be here today."

"I THINK THAT SHOULD BE THE NEXT CIVIL RIGHTS MOVEMENT; BAN THE ASSAULT WEAPONS SO THAT OUR BABIES CAN BE SAFE."

SERENA WILLIAMS

1981–PRESENT

HER SUPERPOWERS:

Mother, sports superstar, role model, ambassador. She's been called the greatest tennis player of all time and it all started with two girls, a racket and one big dream.

HER INCREDIBLE STORY

It's hard to imagine the tennis world without Serena Williams. She's not just "one of the best female tennis players of our time", she's one of the best tennis players of all time. And that's no exaggeration.

This queen has dominated international tennis for decades and is still going strong. Ranked No. 1 countless times by the World Tennis Association, Serena has owned the court alone and also played victoriously with her beloved sister, Venus. She's earned 72 championship titles, landed the most Grand Slam titles ever and has won 88 per cent of the career matches she's played. It's safe to say she's one heck of a total tennis boss.

But being a world-renowned black female tennis player isn't without its struggles. For 14 years, Serena had to boycott the Indian Wells tournament after the crowd jeered and made racist comments to her dad in 2001. She's been illustrated as an angry black monster numerous times for daring to speak her mind. She's had her comfortable, modest tennis outfits banned in favour of traditional tiny tennis skirts. And she's constantly told she's "too big" for having muscles that men would be praised for.

But the more people have tried to bring this wonder lady down, the more she's spoken up. Serena, who was raised a Jehovah's Witness and taught to play tennis by her father, has amplified her voice against prejudice and let no hater diminish her world-class achievements and all-round awesomeness.

In 2015, a new chapter of her life began while she was visiting for the Italian Open. She was having brunch at a hotel when she got chatting to Alexis Ohanian, founder of Reddit. He'd never seen a tennis match and she'd never heard of Reddit, but opposites attract, right? The next day, he came to see her play and the rest is history.

Alexis proposed in December 2016. And a month later, Serena kicked off the new year by handing him a paper bag filled with six positive pregnancy tests. They got married that November with Serena's sister, Venus, by her side and their gorgeous two-month-old baby in her arms.

Just a month before their fairytale wedding, Serena was fighting for her life in hospital after giving birth to baby Alexis Olympia Ohanian Jr. She's since opened up about her frightening labour, and spoken out about postpartum depression and motherhood multi-tasking – think breast pumping in the locker room before an international match.

Having experienced racism, sexism and scrutiny her whole career, Serena uses her voice to invoke change. She regularly speaks out about topics like the gender pay gap and the media's one-dimensional portrayal of "beauty". No matter what happens in her life now, she feels she's "already won" with beautiful baby Alexis Olympia. What a hero.

HER AWESOME ACHIEVEMENTS

➔ Seven times Wimbledon singles champion.

➔ She and her sister were the first team to win three gold medals in women's doubles.

➔ Her charitable foundation created the Serena Williams Secondary School in Kenya. They also provide college scholarships to underprivileged young people.

➔ For most tennis players, 30 is retirement age. But not for Serena, who has broken records as the only tennis player to ever complete the career Grand Slam over the age of 30.

➔ First African-American person to win the Australian Open in 2003.

"WE MUST CONTINUE TO DREAM BIG, AND IN DOING SO, WE EMPOWER THE NEXT GENERATION OF WOMEN TO BE JUST AS BOLD IN THEIR PURSUITS."

SOJOURNER TRUTH

C.1797–1883

HER SUPERPOWERS:

She grew up in slavery and went on to fight for equality and women's rights. Sojourner Truth was special.

HER INCREDIBLE STORY

A hundred dollars and a flock of sheep – that's what Sojourner Truth (born Isabelle Baumfree) was traded for as a slave in 1806. At just nine years old, she found herself owned by a violent man named John Needy, who beat her daily. By the time she was 11, she'd been sold twice more and was living in West Park, New York as property of John Dumont.

Glimmers of home and happiness emerged when Sojourner fell in love with a slave named Robert in 1815, but Robert's owner disapproved of the relationship. One night, when he snuck out to meet Sojourner, his owner beat him so savagely that he died from the injuries years later. She was heartbroken and didn't love again for years.

Slavery was eventually abolished but Sojourner's owner refused to grant her freedom. So she decided to escape with her baby, although, heartbreakingly, this meant leaving her five-year-old son behind. Sojourner found safety for herself and her daughter, but her son wasn't so fortunate. It came to light that he'd been sold to a plantation in Alabama and was being abused. This absolutely devastated Sojourner.

Despite not being able to read or write, she took the issue to court and became the first black woman to win a court case against a white man. It was a huge achievement and it meant that she got her son back. The victory empowered her to start empowering others. She began to travel the country, advocating women's rights and the abolishment of slavery everywhere.

Finally free, she bought a house of her very own in 1850 where she shared her story with good friend Olive Gilbert. Her memoir was published as *The Narrative of Sojourner Truth: A Northern Slave* and Truth used the profits to pay off the mortgage.

Over the years, she gave countless speeches on equality and women's rights. The most famous was her 1851 speech at Ohio Women's Rights Convention, titled "Ain't I a Woman?", where she argued that women had proven they were just as strong and capable as men and deserved the same rights. She commanded the audience with a powerful and confident presence that was so rare at the time that people began to question if she was a woman. When asked this during a speech, she's believed to have opened her blouse and shown her breasts.

Her incredible work continued until her death in 1883. This wonder woman protested for former slaves to be given land they could build homes on. She called for the desegregation of streetcars and met all resistance with tenacity and determination. She can be remembered as an amazing activist, whose hard work paved the ways for centuries of advances in women's rights.

HER AWESOME ACHIEVEMENTS

→ Once risked her life singing at a "mob of wild young men" who threatened to burn the tents at a meeting she was speaking at. It worked and they left after they bargained for "one more song".

→ Inducted into the National Women's Hall of Fame in New York, 1981.

→ NASA named Mars Pathfinder's robotic rover after Sojourner in 1993.

→ The first black woman honoured with a bust in the US Capitol.

→ Has several schools named after her in numerous different US states.

"I HAVE PLOUGHED AND PLANTED, AND GATHERED INTO BARNS, AND NO MAN COULD HEAD ME! AND AIN'T I A WOMAN? I COULD WORK AS MUCH AND EAT AS MUCH AS A MAN... WHEN I GET IT... AND BEAR THE LASH AS WELL. AND AIN'T I A WOMAN?"

TESSA SANDERSON

1956–PRESENT

HER SUPERPOWERS:

Sports queen Tessa Sanderson was the first British black woman to win Olympic gold.

HER INCREDIBLE STORY

Trading in the tropics of the Caribbean for the English city of Wolverhampton might not seem the like easiest move in the world but Tessa Sanderson took it, quite literally, in her stride.

She moved to the UK from Jamaica aged six and settled into Midlands life by throwing herself into sports. Athletics became her favourite hobby and it wasn't long before she was wowing mums and dads in school competitions. As a teen, Tessa joined the Wolverhampton & Bilston Athletic Club and became their star javelin thrower and pentathlete. She set a number of junior records before being tapped up for bigger competitions.

As her sporting success was hitting new heights, Tessa was enduring vile racism in her local area. She remembers being spat on and called a "golliwog" and the n-word. It was incredibly "hurtful" but she didn't let people's ignorance and horrible racist views hold her back from doing what she loved.

In 1976, she represented Great Britain in the javelin at the Olympic Games in Montreal. She finished tenth and was the youngest competitor to reach the finals. Her performance just kept getting better and better and, in 1978, she became the first British woman to win the javelin event at the Commonwealth Games in 16 years, out-throwing her competition by 7 metres. She won gold at the Commonwealth Games again in 1986 and 1990.

Never one to shy away from a sporting challenge, Tessa competed in every Olympics between 1976 and 1996. Her dreams came true in 1984, when she became the first black British woman to win Olympic gold – and the first (and to date, only) British woman ever to win gold for javelin. And they say girls can't throw!

She retired from competing in 1997 but she's been heavily involved in sports ever since. For years, she ran the Newham Sports Academy that helped athletes train to compete in the 2012 Olympic and Paralympic games. She also served as Vice Chairperson of Sport England and founded her own charity, the Tessa Sanderson Foundation and Academy, to help young disabled and non-disabled athletes achieve their sporting goals. These are just a couple of the many things she's done to give back to the community she cares deeply about. It hasn't gone unnoticed either: this six-time Olympian has gone from MBE to OBE to CBE and even snapped up the *Sunday Times* Lifetime Achievement Award.

And among all of her incredible work, she found time to arrange a wedding! She married judo champion Densign White in 2010, with her Olympic team mates Sharron Davies, Kelly Holmes and Christine Ohuruogu as her bridesmaids. Shortly after, in 2013, the couple adopted beautiful twins Cassius and Ruby Mae, then four months old. "They are our world", Tessa says.

What a queen! Sixty is totally the new 50.

HER AWESOME ACHIEVEMENTS

→ Received an MBE, OBE and most recently, in 2014, a CBE.

→ Started modelling at 60 – and looked amazing (as ever).

→ Has a housing estate (Sanderson Park) named after her in her old hometown.

→ Won gold at three Commonwealth Games (1978, 1986, 1990).

→ First black woman to win an Olympic gold, Los Angeles 1984.

"I DID EVERY DAMN THING I WANTED TO DO. I LOVED GETTING DRESSED UP AND GOING OUT WITH THE GIRLS."

"IT'S BEEN A TOUGH JOURNEY BUT THE GIRL DONE GOOD."

WINNIE HARLOW

1994–PRESENT

HER SUPERPOWERS:

Winnie Harlow. She's taken the modelling industry by storm – and is as inspirational as she is beautiful.

HER INCREDIBLE STORY

From gorgeous holidays to global runways, her Instagram feed shows off just the lifestyle you'd expect from a worldwide supermodel. But it hasn't always been sunshine and smiles for Winnie Harlow. Born Chantelle Brown-Young, Winnie suffered toxic bullying in her earlier years. She was branded a "cow", a "zebra" and other disparaging things – all because of the beautiful colours of her skin.

Diagnosed with vitiligo at four years old, Winnie's skin colour started to change rapidly and took on stunning marbled shades of light and dark. Her early school years were filled with verbal and physical abuse and daily choruses of "moo". Outcast for "looking different", she remembers feeling suicidal and wishing her skin condition away. It wasn't until she moved to her third school, at 16, that her confidence started to boost. Having left the bullies behind, Winnie's grades started to soar and she got a job in a local call centre. Then, out of the blue, a journalist contacted her on Facebook, telling her she was "strikingly beautiful" and should try modelling. It was something she'd never thought about before but she gave it a go.

With her modelling ambition in mind, Winnie snapped up the chance to go along to *America's Next Top Model* fashion show when it came to a town nearby. She even built up the confidence to say hi to some contestants and was super surprised when they gathered around her, showering her in compliments and telling her how "gorgeous" she was. It was just the encouragement she needed. Winnie started walking for local catwalk shows and tagging Tyra Banks in Instagram posts in a hope that she'd notice. It paid off and a casting director for *America's Next Top Model* contacted Winnie to audition. Although she made the cut, she didn't win. But she didn't need to. After stunning millions of viewers, Winnie left the show inundated with famous names wanting to work with her.

Today, she's a runway queen and cover girl head turner with a list of successes as long as her legs. She's walked the same catwalks as Naomi, been photographed on every continent for huge-name brands, and her biggest fans include Serena Williams, Drake and Lewis Hamilton. Did we mention that she was handpicked by Beyoncé to feature in her first visual album?

And she still made time to go back to the school she was bullied at to talk to students about being kind to each other. From TED talks to tweets, Winnie uses her experience to inspire people to love their unique beauty. So next time you're feeling down or hung up on other people's unkindness, think of this lady. Pick yourself up, remember you're fabulous and strut your hot stuff.

HER AWESOME ACHIEVEMENTS

➔ Won *Glamour* magazine Editor's Award in 2017.

➔ Has a starring role in Beyoncé's visual album, *Lemonade.*

➔ Delivered a TED talk on "Living With Vitiligo" in 2014.

➔ Chosen to be a Victoria's Secrets model in 2018 (cried with happiness when she found out).

➔ The first and only Canadian to star in *America's Next Top Model.*

"I USED TO FEEL I HAD LOW SELF-ESTEEM OR I WASN'T THE PRETTIEST GIRL. BUT I REALIZED THAT WASN'T REALLY MY OPINION OF MYSELF. I WAS JUST PAYING ATTENTION TO WHAT OTHER PEOPLE WERE SAYING. I HAD TO SIT MYSELF DOWN AND BE LIKE, 'I ACTUALLY DON'T FEEL THAT WAY AND WHATEVER THEY SAY REALLY ISN'T RELEVANT'."

YEONMI PARK

1993–PRESENT

HER SUPERPOWERS:

Her story pulls on the heartstrings. It's a tale of breathtaking bravery and harrowing honesty – one that should never be forgotten.

HER INCREDIBLE STORY

Yeonmi Park has been through an unimaginable journey.

She was born in 1993 in a small town in North Korea. Growing up under the tyrannical Kim Jong-il dictatorship, Yeonmi witnessed the horrors first-hand. She saw bodies piled in rubbish heaps, babies left crying in the street and people executed simply for watching a Hollywood film. When her father was sent to a labour camp for metal smuggling, Yeonmi, her mother and her sister were forced to eat grasshoppers and dragonflies to stay alive.

Her father was eventually released in 2003, and he urged them to escape. Yeonmi's sister, Eunmi, went immediately and, worried that they'd be punished for her escape, the family asked traffickers to help them escape to China. They walked for miles, crossing a frozen river and three mountains to get to the Chinese border. Yeonmi's father grew ill en route and, not wanting to slow them down, decided to stay behind.

The family were met with traffickers when they finally reached the border. One tried to rape Yeonmi and threatened to alert the authorities if she didn't comply. Yeonmi's mother offered herself instead and Yeonmi was forced to watch as it happened. Yeonmi's father was eventually smuggled over the border but died of colon cancer shortly after. The two ladies had to bury him in silence, in the dark of the night.

Just when they were about to give up hope, Yeonmi and her mother met a woman who told them that South Korea may grant them refugee status. They braved near-freezing conditions to reach the China–Mongolia border. When they got there, they were challenged by guards. Both Yeonmi and her mother drew knives and said their goodbyes, willing to kill themselves rather than be sent back. The guards saw the desperation in their eyes and let them enter.

In 2009, Yeonmi and her mother finally found safety in South Korea. They reunited with Eumni five years later – seven years since they'd last seen her. Finally at peace, Yeonmi began to share her story. In 2014, she stunned the entire audience with her story at the One Young World Summit speech and moved to America shortly afterwards to write her memoir and study at university.

It's a happy ending to a story of heartache. A story that's seen one girl "shine a light on the darkest place in the world". As well as bravely sharing her own experience, Yeonmi is a member of numerous programmes to support other refugees from North Korea and encourage the world to help protect human rights in the country. Now married with a son, she hopes to rebury her father's ashes one day and to live to see freedom for North Korea. We really hope so too.

HER AWESOME ACHIEVEMENTS

➜ Co-hosted podcast North Korea Today, discussing the life of refugees after their escape.

➜ Her powerful speech at the One Young World Summit in 2014 received 50 million views in two days.

➜ Her book, *In Order to Live: A North Korean Girl's Journey to Freedom*, was published in 2015.

➜ Member of LiNK (Liberty in North Korea), a non-profit organization that rescues North Korean refugees hiding in China and helps resettle them to South Korea and the US.

➜ Raised thousands of dollars in support of human rights causes.

"ALONG MY JOURNEY, I HAVE SEEN THE HORRORS THAT HUMANS CAN INFLICT ON ONE ANOTHER, BUT I'VE ALSO WITNESSED ACTS OF TENDERNESS AND KINDNESS AND SACRIFICE IN THE WORST IMAGINABLE CIRCUMSTANCES."

BOOK CLUB QUESTIONS

→ Who were your top three favourite iconic women and why?

→ If you could live a day in any of these women's lives, who would it be?

→ Which part made you laugh the loudest?

→ If you could go for a coffee and a chat with any of these iconic women, who would it be and why?

→ Which of these women would you love to party with and why?

→ Which of the themes in this book are still affecting women today, and to what extent?

→ Which part tugged on your heartstrings the most?

→ What main lesson can we learn today from these iconic women?

FURTHER READING

I Put a Spell on You: The Autobiography by Nina Simone

Noughts and Crosses – a novel series by Malorie Blackman

What a Time to Be Alone by Chidera Eggerue

Americanah by Chimamanda Ngozie Adichie

I Know Why the Caged Bird Sings by Maya Angelou

Fierce Fairytales by Nikita Gill

And Still I Rise: A Mother's Search for Justice by Doreen Lawrence

In Order to Live: A North Korean Girl's Journey to Freedom by Yeonmi Park

I Am Malala: The Girl who Stood Up for Education and was Shot by the Taliban by Malala Yousafzai and Christina Lamb

The Colour Purple by Alice Walker

What I Know for Sure by Oprah Winfrey

Collages by Lorna Simpson

Rosa Parks: My Story by Rosa Parks and Jim Haskins

Through My Eyes by Ruby Bridges

Becoming by Michelle Obama

Find Where the Wind Goes by Mae Jemison

My Life: Queen of the Court by Serena Williams

Have you enjoyed this book?
If so, why not write a review on
your favourite website?

If you're interested in finding out more
about our books, find us on Facebook
at **Summersdale Publishers** and follow
us on Twitter at **@Summersdale**.

Thanks very much for buying
this Summersdale book.

www.summersdale.com